# Putting Big Sticks by Little Sticks

# Putting Big Sticks by Little Sticks

## Finding my Path as a Land Surveyor

# Ronald J. Nelms

Published by BookBaby
www.bookbaby.com

Cover and book design by Tony Monaco

First Published 2021

Manufactured in the United States

ISBN: 978-1667821290

*Dedicated to:*

My grandsons Thomas, Matiaus, and Henry;
Granddaughter Alys;
and my adopted grandson Christopher

May your thirst for wisdom be satisfied by
the deep waters that lie within you.

# Editor's Note:

My friendship with Ron began when our company rented a section of his business building. He was a help to us. I was just into my retirement years, and noted that this pleasant fellow was trying to keep his family together but losing bit by bit. He shared his story with me, and I used my background as a published writer and counselor to edit his manuscript. We exchanged views about both the disappointments that break-up families, but also the glories of success in professional life taken with the ideals of an intellectual/ faith life. In the course of years of writing Ron emerged with exactly what I was hoping for. The experience of understanding his own life story led to faith that his life could achieve personal application to pleasant maturity and achievement that is fulfilling.

Dr. Mark Lee

"There is no greater agony than bearing
an untold story inside you"

Maya Angelou

# Contents

# Putting Big Sticks by Little Sticks

## Foreword:

As he gives us a peek into his professional life and the fulfillment he's found in his land surveying career, Ron Nelms retraces his path from childhood adventures through to challenges and tragedies of young adulthood and, ultimately, discovery of the personal gifts that led him to the professional love of his life: land surveying.

*Putting Big Sticks by Little Sticks* is more than a story about a land surveyor who found his passion. It's a memoir of a boy and his dog, brotherly love, and the mischievous adventures that call to those anxious to explore woods, hills, abandoned mines and ladybug dens. It's a story of family resilience, trust, and faith, and the role each has had in Ron's life.

Youth is short-lived, and little boys enjoy precious few years of carefree play and exploration before getting to the task of school, growing up, and starting a family and career. If they're lucky, they will find a life's work that fills them up, bringing both joy and pride, all while being a "servant to others," as Ron describes his work and the responsibility that comes with it.

Ron Nelms is one of the lucky ones. Life as a professional land surveyor has been his dream come true. No matter what your personal calling may be, Ron's story inspires us to lean into our God given gifts and to put them to work in our life.

Cheryl M. Scott

Preface

*Preface*

My life is blessed in many ways and at the top of the list are my two sons Tyler and Aaron. Both have their different talents. Tyler is quick witted with a great sense of humor. He also has a keen eye on taking photographs that capture the essence of what he is attempting to communicate. His hobby includes the ability to paint with precision tiny figurines that essentially have parts that are no bigger than the head of a needle. They inspire me to write about their father when they have so much time for life left.

My other son Aaron has a bit of a dry sarcastic humor and has a talent to do finish work of construction projects. He has the patience to measure with precision the exact cut needed to fit the pieces together. Without much education in physics, he is still able to understand structural integrity.

Both of them have talents that are far different than my own. When Aaron was around 15, we purchased four acres in the Glennville area which is 40 miles northeast of Bakersfield, California. Living so far out of town meant you had to make sure you picked up everything you needed before leaving Bakersfield. Missing a few bolts could hold up the project until you got back to town.

Shortly after purchasing the property, we decided that we needed a shed to store supplies. So Aaron and I stopped at Lowe's to buy a fully equipped shed with all the parts needed to assemble. All we had to do was put it together. We opened up the box and separated the items on the ground. But there was no floor. Befuddled, I looked at Aaron and asked do you see the part for the floor? He looked back in disbelief that I would even ask such a question but not wanting demonstrate disrespect, he answered, "Dad, you have to pour a concrete floor for it to sit on." My response was along the line of well they shouldn't advertise it as "all the parts to assemble" on the box.

At that point I was determined that we were going to get this shed up and not wait another weekend. So, we found scraps of 2"x4" boards and odds and ends of plywood some ¾" thick and others ½" thick. It was the worst assembled shed you could image. The whole time we were constructing Aaron would let out little groans but at the time I shrugged them off because he was only a teenager. When completed it stood but wobbled and in reality it probably wouldn't stand up to a significant wind storm.

For the next year every time we would pass the shed on the trip home, Aaron would let out a groan and shiver until one day I asked him if he was OK. He replied, "Dad, I will make a deal with you. You buy the supplies for a new shed and I will build you a new one but under one condition."

My thoughts were that it would be a good project for him and the worst that could happen is the loss of material. "OK, but what is the condition?"

"You don't help me."

I was a bit stunned but I agreed to the terms. He then proceeded to build me a shed like no other.

It was solid. The walls were perfect 90 degrees, the studs spaced properly, and the roof was leak proof. And it didn't move when I pushed on it.

During my life it has been my experience that the majority of people I encounter do not enjoy their job. When I say "enjoy" I mean **ENJOY** to a sense of passion where you work not just for the paycheck but for the satisfaction that it has purpose and meaning. Often times one settles for something less than what they envisioned themselves being. Not necessarily a bad thing. Most fall into their position with little regard to the journey. When at your job and its 5 minutes to quitting time, do you say 'almost there'? If that is the case then you are not enjoying your job and probably should look for something else to do.

# Preface

I was in that situation but fortunately I realized it at an early age and was able to change. That has made all the difference. But there was a struggle *looking for a career in all the wrong places* (yes, a play on the song). Starting as a dishwasher then a short order cook, in between I worked park maintenance, and I set up mobile homes. But through it all it led me to a fulfilling profession.

Life is a struggle but when embraced one begins to recognize there are reasons for all of it. Then the rewards begin to come in. One thing I have learned is to not fear because it only brings paralysis and immobilization. Always look for opportunities and most importantly take note of the things that draw your attention. Find the grit to press on.

Tragedies occur but we are measured by how we transcend to rise above the circumstances and use them for good. Sometimes we win and sometimes we lose but through it all if taken in perspective we find what it is we like to do. The point of it all is right thought and faith.

Each person has his or her own story, of how they found their career. It may be overcoming poverty or adversity through family life. Maybe they knew what they wanted from the beginning. But I believe each of us has a divine gift that is built inside each of us. Many times it is hidden and needs to be drawn out of deep waters. It will not always be easy or pleasant but if searched for with diligence the consequences are worth the effort.

As a Land Surveyor, often times I am required to read plans and documents then mark their location on the ground. They could be property lines, buildings, utilities, and easements to name a few. These markers could be anything from wood hubs to iron pipes. They could either be set or found. Generally, they are small in size measuring from half inch to 6 inches in diameter. Usually they are flush or below the surface and not clearly visible. In order to make them identifiable we put a taller marker next to it usually four feet in height.

I heard a story once about a surveyor who marked a property line then handed the bill to the client. His response was "That's a lot for a couple of sticks!"

What I do is put big sticks by little sticks. While reflecting on life I determined I love what I do and am extremely fortunate to have found a career that brings me fulfillment. So I began putting the sticks together.

The following pages comprise my remembrance of a journey in finding my gift as a land surveyor. Perhaps readers will be inspired to discover what they like to do and these words encourage them to search and reflect. Throughout my life, I have had the privilege of having wonderful mentors who probably did not realize the affect they had. Perhaps you are a mentor. Hopefully, this book will assist you in recognizing the gifts both in you and in others. I pray to have been useful to family and others. That is necessary to life for leadership in the highs and lows we all pass through. The following pages comprise my remembrance of a journey in finding my gift as a land surveyor and how I put the Big Sticks by the Little Sticks.

## *Fun in the Street*

The father did think it would be fun
To take the boys for a run
They gathered in the truck at the morning sun
Instructions were given and spun

When they arrived at the site
All was ready because seemed right
That they could complete this duty before the night

Each received a bright orange vest
For that seemed to be best
Protection was important to give dad rest
Below the knees it hung on the older

# Preface

And to the road as it pleased on the younger
To be dressed this way should have brought much laughter
But father only smiled at such a family matter

The father was concerned of the traffic that day
But it turned out they could walk as they may
For vehicles were scarce to be found
Which meant his decision was sound

Out to the middle of the street they strode
With a shovel, hammer, and metal goad
It was a monument they needed to find
For it would keep the neighbors kind

The boys were excited to tear up the street
Because they thought there could be no better treat
Than to do something on the spot
That normally they could not

The older held the goad
While father tapped it into the road
Around in a circle they did go
Until able to pop up the foe

Under the hard asphalt did lay
The dirt which was soft this day
The younger grabbed the shovel for his play

They dug through the soil searching for the treasure
It was no dreary task but was a pleasure
To be digging in a place where safety was unsure
Especially when dad was there to reassure

The three did not have to work long in this feat
For they soon found the monument in its seat
The measurement made it complete
As they went on to the next street

Putting Big Sticks by Little Sticks

# 1
# *Early Explorations*

*"Felix, qui potuit rerum cognoscere causas."*
– *"Fortunate is he who understands the cause of things."*

For virtually all normal persons there appear within, affinities and talents that seek, perhaps await, attention and expression. We have to grow a bit before they begin to reveal themselves in a meaningful manageable way. They may show up early in life. Many magicians were child prodigies. The meaning and nature of gifts press upon us for recognition and cultivation. They are a part of us and influence our lives to some degree even when we do not recognize them. When they are rightly understood and managed, they are enlarged. Neglected they tend to fall away. Sometimes others see gifts in us and we do not.

Cultivated, human gifts enlarge, and become more meaningful, more fulfilling. Some mentoring, especially in the involvement of parents, moves matters along with helpful dispatch. This is commonly illustrated in the accomplishment of athletes in the Olympics (and elsewhere) when parents and coaches are often honored for what they contributed in the lives of masterful young men and women showing physical prowess. Both the mentor and the athlete seem to have improved the other in some way. Approval from respected persons in our lives, in the maturing process, inspires improvement. It is key to effective parenting. We sometimes call it mentoring. It is a special relationship. It is another way to reproduce ourselves.

Human affinities long to be expressed. Often they are repressed either by the individual or by others in the contexts of life. Many a young person has been told he or she will not amount to anything. Some parents invite their children to defeat. Efforts are discouraged. Attempts are aborted. Young persons may turn to some of their peers in using time for lesser purposes and activities, shallow for the hidden potential, and less satisfying to their view of life and the world. Some may juggle with dreams for a lifetime, perhaps fritter their talents away. Others know early on and press for fulfillment of some meaningful vision. Some follow through, activating themselves toward their dreams and felt abilities. A young person is blessed when parents and/ or mentors enter into his or her life in a way to advance the achievement of constructive dreams. The helper lowers barriers, and strengthens to some degree the protégé who must accomplish the better part of the possibilities. Some parents see the spark in their children – and water it. Others find some fuel for the flame. They may make possibilities into probabilities.

For me the dream came early, even if it was a bit murky – as it usually is for a child. Now, reflecting back, I see the early seeds of my dreams. I discovered I wanted something that would give me adventure. Some persons never find a spark for their lives. No one shows up to encourage and advance the search. We know that there are persons who have felt a drive, but nothing came of the first evidences of affinities looking toward gifts of wisdom or resources and developed skills needed to accomplish a dream. I wanted to look beyond the limits I felt were the outlines of current life. Was there something yet to conquer? Who lives over there? What treasure may be found? How does one get there? What does everything look like in places I have never been? It was a thirst for exploration and adventure, both near and far, both in fantasy and reality. The thoughts did not reach beyond possibilities. Dreams are not all fantasies. They can become the inspiration to life's journey.

My earliest recall, at the age of four, relates to standing in our family living room ruminating about a painting mounted on the wall. I now know that I was taken by the oblique view of a cliff surrounded by trees of pine and cedar. The rendition was at odds with my environment. Our home fronted on a side street that ran parallel to the main highway from the Central Valley to Grass Valley in the mountains of California. My brothers and I, somewhat rebellious in childishness, were instructed firmly not to play in the back yard, so to avoid the cut bank that overlooked that busy route. In something of innocent defiance, common to kids, I set out to discover what the cliff looked like, and what discoveries might be made related to the massive project. However, the back door was locked so to bar us from the backyard, and the intrusive highway. I was never fully free to make my foray to that frontier. I was infected with desire that was intensified by a locked door.

The route to adventure was blocked. I pondered the painting in the front room. It seemed to me the secret to my venture might be hidden there. Although no answer came to me at the time, I was somewhat comforted that the cut bank and the oblique cliff of the painting were related – at least for my thoughts. To find the secret to the one might provide the secret to the other. Why would the cut-bank be bad, and the cliff be worthy of an honored place on our wall? I wanted to know what was back of this extension, and the mystery of the locked door and forbidden yard – a yard that grown-ups might use on occasion through a guarded door. There had to be an answer. To satisfy my yearning I made the painting to be the cut-bank, and permitted it to become my answer. My yearning about exploring the cut-bank was unrequited in reality. My urgings had to be muted, but they were real. Adventure was beginning in my imagination.

In family course, we moved to Union Hill, a mountain community east of Grass Valley. The beauties of the cliff painting suddenly looked real, and may have accounted for some of my memory, imagining about the cut-bank, a mere symbol for real beauty in nature. I became more aware of reality in the passing of time. With some bravado, and growing in both body and perceptions I announced to my mother that I was going to explore our new location. Our dog, Peanut, would be my companion. The safer community environment and my growing-up were enough for her to set me free, at least for the present. She was not privy to my plans. She didn't ask.

Peanut and I took off through the woods behind our recently acquired but modest home. The dog seemed brave enough and so was I. Exploration began. I knew I was in my element. I was becoming what I wanted to be in some relationship with the mysteries of nature – real and imagined. Explorations continued. Each time I would look for a new trail, and master the old ones. Following each to its destination, I wondered why the trail was located here and looked for evidence of man or animal, proofs of persons or pets that traveled this way. I was intrigued, somewhat overwhelmed in my imagination of the unknown in the known.

From time to time I would find narrow slants of wood, decorated with colorful ribbons. They were sometimes irresistible. I would lift some of them out of the ground, toss them in the air, and watch the fluttering of ribbon in the fallback. I had no knowledge that these were surveyor sticks used to mark boundaries, or the perimeter of a timber sale. I wonder if I were to return to those old trails, the voices of some surveyors may be groaning at me as the ghost of old Marley groaned at Scrooge. The voices would rise from the graves in unison berating me for my disregard for the meaning of ribboned sticks. (I have been amply punished for my childish delinquency in adult life when, as a surveyor I have lost many sticks to venturesome persons taken by fluttering ribbons.) I hope the offenders were children.

On one occasion, my younger brother, Dean and I, with Peanut, trudged up a trail to the top of a cut bank. It overlooked a saw mill. Trucks moved in slow, laborious but smooth routings into and out of the area, unloading fresh and rough timber, and loading treated logs or cut lumber. The hum of the saw blades was clear, interrupted by beginnings and endings of the cutting rhythm dictated by the length of the log in transition to lumber. The sounds from the energy of the motor recited the nature and length of each log in the surgery of it. The workers seemed like a part the mechanics of the process, moving with clear purpose to the various points in the scene of the great compound. Their meaning to it all was everything to the composition of the scene. I was entranced. There was adventure in it for me.

I studied the scene in my imagination of my young mind. The composition was magnificent. We felt we had discovered some secret operation. It was reality, visited by some vision or dream that belongs to human beings. Some don't catch it. It is a tuning into real life. Tuning in we discover something for ourselves, to contribute to our purpose on the world's compound for self and mankind, useful for all in the context - whether highly gifted or modestly engaged. Somewhere there is something meaningful for each person. It must be sought to be made practical. We are invited to discover who we are and what we want to accomplish in life. I felt that adventure early in my dreams. I wish that a wise mentor might have caught up with me – and Peanut.

So intriguing was the moving scene that I wanted to get closer. I stepped off the pathway, and pressed through the underbrush to a clearing only yards or so away from the mill's activity. Going forward a bit, I slipped and my legs were pinned against and under a decaying log. The accident disturbed a nest of lady bugs. (And, hereto hangs a long tale of comparisons and contrasts in my life story – some of which my reader will encounter later in this narrative.) Pets had invaded my dream, even if Peanut held my first loyalty.

The log was home for the lady bugs, and they seemed disturbed that their peaceful existence had been so summarily interrupted. I was somewhat immobile, and engulfed by thousands of these insects, insects usually docile. They filled the air, fluttering about, and landing wherever they could - including on my body. Their kingdom had been invaded, but they had no effective weapons to subdue the intruder. My first reaction was fear, but I soon remembered that these bugs were harmless to humans, even if they were a threat to other bugs harmful to mankind. I even felt some delight in observing them in their trial to settle down. Their activity tickled my skin. With help from Dean, I wriggled out of the encompassing log. We agreed that this log might be the place of the origin of lady bugs, their Eden. Our discovery was not to be treated lightly, and we had some responsibility for this divine information. We just didn't know what to do with it. The bugs didn't either.

As uninvited interlopers in this magnificent scene, we did not want to be observed by the mill workers, and we felt protective of the lady bugs. What would those big men do to lady bugs messing with forest logs? The bugs could only be protected by our silence. We agreed to secret silence to all persons about our encounter with the bugs. Our concern was to extricate ourselves without being caught. No one seemed to have observed the disturbance of the lady bugs, or noticed my predicament. Feeling confident of our privacy, I gently removed the silent, clinging bugs, returning them one by one to their nest. Peanut looked on with a placid curiosity, but did not betray our situation. A bark would have revealed that he was in favor of the big guys of the mill.

Animated we briskly headed home, excited by our lady bug safari. We wanted to avoid the workers so as to escape judgment for intrusion, but we also wanted to confide with mother about our findings for she was the one person who knew everything, particularly in regards to divine information and the fair communication thereof. Perceiving our purpose, Peanut joined us in our report, barking out, in his approving and repetitive language, our findings. Mother's take on the whole matter was different than ours. She was surprised at us walking several miles through the woods and scolded us for walking so far from home without an older partner. As far as the lady bugs, she comforted us by telling us that the lady bugs were in a good location and God would take care of them. The scolding called us to safety, and the future of the lady bugs was in competent Divine Hands. Mother would keep our secret, showing the loyalty of mothers to their children, and especially against the lady-bug police. We relaxed in learning that all was and will be well. Mothers can do that for kids. They deserve medals – or something.

Even so, a few days later when the scolding had worn off, we went back to the site of adventure, only to experience disappointment. The lady bugs were gone, the mill was silent, the secret operation of the mill had ceased. We must have chosen a day off for the crew. We were grieved, even Peanut seemed grieved. Had we inadvertently betrayed the lady bugs location to the mill workers and they disposed of them? Were we negligent in our responsibilities to the divine Master? All we could do was express our concern to our mother. This time Mother was not scolding but assuring. She explained that it was likely that the bugs felt danger in that location and moved on to a better home that might be kept secret from marauding boys and dogs.

There was much more for me during those Tom Sawyer/Huck Finn days. Some hikes provided blackberry bushes, fig and apple trees. There was too much for a boy and a dog so we found ways to share the bounty with friends and family. There were moments of danger as when we boys came across a bee hive. One of my ambitious friends decided to knock it to the ground.

He was promptly punished with a number of stings. It was then that things really began to look bleak, as he announced that he was allergic to bee stings, and required immediate medical attention. By this time I was old enough to evaluate the situation so to determine a course of action. To return with him would be to leave a significant honey comb, but we also had concern for his welfare. We quickly determined to send him back home with one of the gang, in case he collapsed; and we would proceed to harvest the treasured honey which, by this time in the fast moving scenario, had been abandoned by the bees. We were thus able to avoid two tragedies, an endangered colleague and an abandoned crop of honey. Either loss seemed tragic.

It was decided that we would share the honey with our wounded friend and his keeper, if the patient survived his stings. It turned out he was not allergic to bee stings, but we were generous in sharing the honey anyway – despite his heinous lies. The honey was delightful and made even better with the addition of peanut butter my mother harvested without much adventure, from a glass jar in the cupboard. With the honey, I had become a contributor to the family welfare. It was clear to me that I was growing up. I may not have been as humble about my achievements as I should have been.

On other explorations, Peanut and I would venture into the nearby Empire State Mine. During this period the mine facility was shut down, but was attractive to adventuresome lads. (Today it is a State Park, but we liked it as a mine.) It was as tempting as a newly found continent for a boy and his dog to investigate. We could follow mine shafts until water created a moat preventing us from entering deeper into the shafts. There were rock separators to climb - conquered if the climber reached the top. They were our 'Mount Everest.' Sometimes we just played through old shacks and buildings on the property. (All this wonderful distraction is now lost to the new century's city kids, even those in the rural communities, in the near complete and pervasive occupation of land and cultural change in society.)

In a short time of self-education I was prepared to offer tours to my friends and explain the features of the mine. We made adventure of it going through unkempt gardens and brush, even pools. There was a formidable clubhouse with a large room that offered mounted animal heads. Some of the heads seemed exotic, causing the young mind to wonder from what distant lands did they come? Even at that age I could tell this had once been a magnificent operation visited by dignitaries of all species. What a discovery, so to play on a youngster's mind. There were fantasies of man and earth that we fabricated. I was in fantasy land. That's not bad for a kid.

To the south of the mine was a sand pit. It seemed like a wasteland. My friends and I wandered through it. We imagined ourselves crossing the desert- perhaps like Lawrence of Arabia leading our troops to victory against impossible elements of nature and implacable troops with little blankets on their heads, held by little ropes crossing their foreheads. During various forays we would slide down some of the slopes, and make a show of it screaming: "Help! I'm slipping into the pit!" Dramatically forming a human chain, we attempted to rescue the vanquished soul only to be sucked downward into the yawning pit. All of us tumbled downward screaming and yelling as if this was leading to the end of our lives. There was a sense of freedom in it all. It was better than Disneyland. What adventure!

At some undesignated moment, someone would yell the enemy is coming. Scrambling back to the top we would retrieve our makeshift guns made of sticks or toy Tommy guns – from Christmas past. We peeked over the sand ridge for the enemy; only to be told that the enemy was behind us. Quickly flopping over the top on the other side we immediately began shooting at our foe making sounds of firing that no respectable Tommy gun would recognize. Feeling that the enemy had our number, we had to either stay and be overcome, or charge. Of course, "Charge!" - was commanded, as every good soldier knew that bravery was on our side for inevitable victory. Down the ridge and then scrambling up the next, each soldier wanted to be the first to reach the top. Jumping and diving with sand flying everywhere, we subdued our imaginary adversary. The adversary just wasn't up to the challenge of the latest Tommy guns.

Our attack on one occasion was interrupted by a cry of impending death due to sand in the eye of one of our gallant warriors. A medic among us was summoned, from whom a corner of his shirt was used to try and remove the offending obstacle, but to no avail. While the victim moaned in agony it was decided that water was needed. A blind soldier would be useless to us.

Because of previous scouting trips I knew that water was available at the clubhouse; therefore I offered to lead our troop to the place of assured recovery. However, aware of the possibility of a grounds keeper in the area, our travel had to be a covert action. Maneuvering our way from tree to bush to tree, we quietly and with thoughtful prowess found our way to the large lawn and the target hospital just beyond. We waited to catch our breath, recover strength, and investigate to make certain the groundskeeper was not in the area. With our wounded comrade still clutching his eye we ran across the grass to the magical faucet. Some of us were assigned to stand guard and watch for the enemy. Others attended to our comrade's eye. We were in the front line of problem solvers. We didn't need Mom, or even Dad, to take care of it.

It was at this point, on the recovery of our wounded comrade that we decided it was time to go home. Besides, it was late, and we were hungry. We had forgotten the C rations for our adventure. There would be time for us to go through new ventures on another day. In all it was a good day. The military victory was obvious; no one had lost his life. The wounded had been cared for, and would live. Bravery had been humbly accepted by all.

It was the stuff a kid's life is made of – if he and she gets a chance. They also have to have imaginations.

*The home I grew up on Union Hill as it is today.*

Putting Big Sticks by Little Sticks

## 2
## *Emerging*

*"Isn't that right Mr. Nelms"*
Mr. Shelton

Union Hill Elementary School was the first school I attended. It was only a few blocks, walking distance, from my home in Grass Valley. The building was constructed as a one room schoolhouse in 1868, nearly a century before I showed up. During the time period I attended (1962-1967) Union Hill had grown to six classrooms and an auditorium. In the northwest corner of the campus and behind the school was the black top area where we would play Kick-ball or Dodge-ball. On occasion Tether-ball would become the sport of choice. On the back lot of the campus was a rock infested baseball diamond. Periodically we would have class outings to remove the emerging nuisances of stones and pebbles. East of the classroom structure and taking up half of the campus was a grassy area that included several stately trees. They provided shaded relief from hard play in the California environment. The site ultimately entered the pleasantries of nostalgia for those of us who were young together – a while ago.

If visiting the site today, you would find those old classrooms still in place. However, there have been added facilities in buildings, offices, and a gymnasium. The school has grown. The landscape has changed somewhat but for me the strong beginnings of a life foundation for intellectual interests and life formation have not changed from the experiences of the old campus. It was there, in a more limited situation that I formed a sound framework even as a child - for my life. At Union Elementary I adopted sportsmanship, embraced education, formed social behaviors, and cultivated imagination – to the degree a child–person of the time might achieve. It was a good beginning in my enlarging world.

Whatever the modern student may receive in the physical improvements of buildings, equipment and various programs, I can hope that the personal interests of the students continues to be cultivated by current teachers as they were for us. Those of my child life period seemed to love us, and that is always at the beginning of a good life in any area of life. That contributed to the quality of instruction, and our response to it. Current news reports suggest that this personal factor has been diluted, perhaps lost in some massive population centers. Only in a few instances do I feel that it could have been improved at Union Hill. One wonders if modern expectations, turns and attitudes have smothered necessary respect for one another at any age. The personal intent and interests play an important role in the maturing and learning processes of life for youngsters. The adults seemed to have a bit of a parenting (caring) attitude for children, but it doesn't get through as fully as it should in current life. At least it doesn't seem so.

Partly because of their personal interest in their growing emerging students, I gained respect for those who, in their assignments, made more than professional effort to nurture young developing minds and persons. On occasion the student felt the interest was in the individual - one student at a time without neglecting any of the others. That takes some doing. I will never forget the master teachers - Mrs. McKitrick, Mrs. Hutsinpiller, and Mrs. Simpson - from my formative educational years. They left lasting, indelible impressions on a boy who loved life and looked forward to the 'grown up' future. They made it their objective, in what now seems to me, to dedicate their lives to these children in human and intellectual formation so to take care, and help them forward to goals of the future. Factors for development would not have entered our minds and conduct. The teachers were instrumental in sparking my interest in reading and understanding the mysteries of the mind, with my specialty mathematics emerging even in my childish imagination. Their mentoring attitudes caused me to realize that learning could be fun and it promised great rewards. The follow-up of those factors in my life prove to me their effectiveness in motivation for learning and doing. I salute them. There is a general concern in current society, if the news reporting represents current educational analysis, that the systems of education in significant large communities of the country have diluted adequate focus on the emerging student. That was not the case for our community fifty years ago. I am grateful. (These statements do not deny that the most excellent students are getting excellent attention for professional life. The best education is for life itself.)

There are fond memories of childhood accomplishment in receiving an A on a spelling or math test. Or the award of stars for some achievement, gold or silver stars to mark acceptable effort, appearing after one's name on the classroom chart for all to see. Even the playground gave us a sense of value. How can anyone express the exultation he or she receives after catching a ball in flight that seals the victory for the team, even if it is just a rag tag team of kids?

With tongue in check, I am reluctant to mention the special honor of being involved in a secret club to defend the oak tree on Union's campus from imaginary foes. I have not heard if the bond of secrecy has been lifted. If not I am here lifting it in the belief that with the passing of nearly fifty years the secrets revealed will not threaten the integrity of our class and the safety of Grass Valley. The foes were imaginary anyway – except for the girls in the Union classes.

Underneath the canopy of a large oak, my buddies and I formed a club called The Hell Cats. We decided to name it after a movie we saw about fighter pilots who flew the "Hell Cat 6F6F" Fighter Plane. The wings would fold up to store better on aircraft carriers. We thought this maneuver was, as the moderns put it: cool. With arms straight out from our sides, imitating an airplane, we made our mission to fly (running at top speeds, same as taxying and flying) and shooting at the girls on campus. After looks of disgust and screams: "Stop it!" We would return to the carrier (the oak tree) where we would fold our fore arms skyward in the same manner as the fighter planes and proclaim: Mission accomplished! It seemed to us that we were winning the war (trumped up to scare the girls, the enemy). On the near surrender of the enemy, our club was admonished and ordered to cease and desist (I believe the order from headquarters was: "Stop It!") Apparently the teachers felt simulation of war activities was not a healthy activity for young boys at a school devoted to peace, especially with families of girls. We were informed that the disruptive crying of terrorized young girls upset the harmonious environment of the playground. After lengthy deliberation that occupied an entire recess period, we soldier buddies decided that we would operate under a more covert fashion in the future. Perhaps we needed a name less threatening – to girls.

My fourth grade teacher, Mr. Jones, seemed to have difficulty holding the classroom's attention. This was his first year teaching. The students sensed his inexperience and would become unruly. As he walked down the aisles calling out: "Quiet!" - He carried a rubber hose piece and rap each desk trying to gain the occupant's attention. On one of these occasions he inadvertently hit my hand. The pain was excruciating, and I yelped. He immediately stopped I could see in his eyes that he realized that his actions were unacceptable, even to him. I felt sorry for him.

My heart was mysteriously touched with compassion for him, and I attempted to hold back the tears that were welling up in my eyes. I realized even at that young age that though his actions were sometimes wrong this grown man was like me, susceptible to making bad decisions. What is important in all is that we learned from them. I did not feel anger or hatred. For a shining moment, I was as a child a teacher of my teacher. He never used the hose again, but frequently he reserved the right to thunder out: "Quiet!" I hear it in the night hours. (Such is the memory of this man from childhood.)

Despite any faults, Jones was enthusiastic about what he did teach – as a true professional seeking to gain educational results from his students. He was passionate about music. One objective was to teach every student how to read a musical score. I admit I couldn't have cared less about the differences between C minor and an F sharp. However, he combined his professional interests for effective purpose. It was through him that I developed and memorized multiplication tables. He would put a record on a phonograph that would begin with a slow cadence asking the answer to multiplication questions such as: "3x5?" followed by a pause – "6x2?" - pause - and the procedure played out. During the pauses we were to write down our answers. When twenty questions were complete, he would check the results. Those scoring 90% or more correct were rewarded by taking another twenty questions where the cadence picked up and if we got those correct we would graduate to the next speed and continue until completed. He speeded up the process, which clicked with me. It was a striking methodology that demanded student attention, and proved to me that learning could be speeded up – if there was interest, aptitude and a means to show what might be accomplished. It became something of a game to win. Each student could become his or her own competition – beating one's own personal time was the way to go.

As my concentration intensified on the math problems at hand, and the situation intensified in the speed up, I felt like I was in a jet airplane attempting to break the sound barrier. Once it was broken, all that was present and needed was the rhythm of the numbers and the pouring out of answers to the paper. The process worked for me. There was a mysterious sense of automatic functioning that seemed to inherit something worthwhile with it. For a period of time I entered into a state of sub-consciousness, oblivious to my surroundings. I became aware of a magical world where mathematics and music were joined. I have been informed that engineers, scientists and mathematicians are commonly drawn to music as their favorite expression of the arts. Math began to take center stage emerging into my favorite subject. We are informed by the analysts that the mind that manages math well is a good thing for the student. In math's mystery for learning the student is aided in other fields. The theory has worked well for me in life and business. It all started for me when I was just a kid. I had no idea as to where it would lead.

It was during the fifth grade year that baseball became another major passion. Mr. Pauley was an athletic sort who promoted sporting activities with an appropriate intensity. He encouraged imagination and reading, particularly in subjects that interested us. Coupling the intellectual and physical served me well. His enthusiasm for sports and my insatiable desire to learn more about it sent me to something of a statistical heaven. I began devouring all the information I could find on America's favorite pastime. I searched through books to find biographies and commentaries on the game.

Fictional novels related to the sport were quickly snatched up. The school's encyclopedia, and Baseball pages were nearly memorized, so to prove my intellectual prowess. I wanted to know the great quartet: hit, run, catch and throw. When I learned about cross referencing, even those pages were studied with intensity. Baseball cards were collected and statistics were poured out from memory. Letters were written to different Major League Baseball teams requesting team photos. Some sent them and others sent order forms. Those sending photos warmed our loyalties. There was sufficient encouragement to keep me going with enthusiasm. America seemed like baseball heaven. And, I had good buddies going there with me.

Late in the night, when I was presumed to be sleeping, I would tune in a small transistor radio, turning the sound low, I would listen to a Giants-Dodgers game. With the speaker to my ear, I imagined the game in my mind following the events just as they happened - perhaps a pitching duel between two greats Juan Marichel and Don Drysdale. With the score tied in the bottom of the ninth and a runner on third with one out, Willie Mays came to the plate. He could have opted to swing for a homerun but risk striking out or hitting a weak grounder if he did set that personal objective. Instead he put his bat on the ball to hit a sacrifice fly to the outfield and win the game by bringing in the lingering base runner. I was reminded again that serving heroics was not usually the better plan. We do best when serving the team. I came to believe in team-work. Mays went out for his team win, not for his personal statistics. (There's that math again.) It is excellent life strategy for a family.

Baseball is a statistical game full of formulas and numbers. Hours were spent on the living room floor scouring the newspaper for the standings, box scores, and schedules. I was intrigued discovering the method of determining an ERA (Earned Run Average), BA (Batting Average), or RBI (Runs Batted In). From these statistics one could speculate the odds of a batter getting a hit off of a particular pitcher. It often turned out just as predicted from the numbers. What better way to practice math – my favorite subject, as my reader may now be persuaded. It is vital to baseball, proving against the advancement of modern mankind over the peasant of the Middle Ages. Baseball beats jousting every time. It also is good practice for math fanatics.

# Emerging

From the living room floor to the ball diamond, I played out my fantasy of being the best baseball player ever. That fantasy is possible for a boy. Statistics would back my claim, at least to myself. Imaginary games were played where I would win the triple crown of home runs, batting average, and runs batted in. Circus catches were performed, as well as running down the ground ball destined for a hit only to be snatched up so to throw out the runner by an eye lash. The only dilemma for my make-believe coach was whether I should play in the field every day or should I be a pitcher every fourth day. (That decision had to be made a century or so ago for (Babe Ruth.) In a pinch with the game on the line, the coach would call on me to get the last outs by striking out the side. Nothing to it, of course, in doing what a person is supposed to do. Dreams can make it happen. It is easy in the dream games of a kid who finds a way to win through imagination. Without imagination persons won't win in either real life or in creativity for future life. To play rightly on the imagination of a child may have more impression for adult life than we may have ever believed. What once lived for us continues to live in some way for adult life to maturity. In imagination we discover how to make life work.

In reality I had a Little League coach, Mr. Peyrot, who was a strong physical man who owned good fatherly characteristics – a great context for a lad. We won the league championships both years I played for him. He made every fellow on the team feel important and made sure all players knew his responsibilities and roles. He instilled the desire to win by fair play and to respect for opponents. There is important learning achieved for life when a youngster has right coaching in everything – from parents and other adults who care and win our attention. In our present hurly-burly lives we seem to have forgotten the value of adult participation in the lives of children emerging to adult life. There is a touch of continuing meaning from the past in it when lost families lose society. It is important that mature persons teach the values of life for ensuing generations.

Small in stature, I did not permit the lack of a few inches deter me from my desire to be a major league baseball player. My claim to fame in Little League was my ability to get on base 27 out of 30 at bats during one season. Twenty six of them were walks. Getting on base was the important thing –

for the team. It helped to crouch and make the strike zone even smaller so more difficult for even a good pitcher to get the batter out. I believe that the twenty six is a record that stands to this day. Of all the baseball statistics that are broken we may not have lost that one –for Little League. It does suggest that you should use what you've got if fairly played out.

Entering the 6th grade, I was pleased to have Mr. Shelton as my teacher. He was also the school's Principal. In addition to those duties he also taught 7th and 8th grades. Everybody seemed to work hard as I remember those days and the experiences. Despite instructing three different grade levels, his management of the classroom was captivating as to how he could keep order and discipline. He was a role model to me in regards to organization and focusing on the tasks at hand. To this day, I believe he had eyes in the back of his head or a rear view mirror secreted in the temples of his glasses. Even with his back turned to us he seemed to know what we were doing. (He just understood kids.)

The sixth graders consisted of about eight students and we took up one row on the left of the classroom. The seventh graders numbered perhaps sixteen students in the middle two rows, while the eighth occupied the two rows on the right. Mr. Shelton would sit behind his desk and rotate at specified times to address the different grade levels. The rule was that while he was instructing one grade the others were to be working on their assignments. We were to keep our heads down and pay attention only to the materials on our own desks. Turning to his right instructing the 8th graders with his back to me and thinking he couldn't see me, I would listen to him instead of doing my work. To which he would address me without turning: "Isn't that right" Mr. Nelms? I was astute enough to know that it was a rhetorical question, and had better pay attention to the work assigned to me and remain silent. I did not reply to his inquisition.

From the first day in his class, I was inspired to organize and to take the necessary time to do homework. He emphasized the importance of being disciplined in completing all assignments. Somehow this gave me a sense of self - worth gained by reaching achievable goals. Not to follow through was to fail oneself – a kind of self- robbery. He was teaching me to be a professional. It also contributed to a sense of growing up, important to maturity.

During these childhood years there was a saintly couple that felt it their calling to educate my brothers and me about personal spiritual issues. I was four years of age when Grace and Andy asked my parents' permission to take my brothers and me to church. My parents, eager for relief of three young toddlers for a couple of hours of leisure, gave enthusiastic approval to the proposal. These caring persons would pick us up on Sunday mornings and take us to Sunday School. We learned the importance of understanding the meaning of faith and the nature of God. This was something like school, but a different context, using some of the same educational systems. Everyone seemed like they cared and wanted something for all of us kids. All this was dependent upon voluntary participation, sometimes uneven. There seems to be blessing in servanthood.

One week each summer the church would sponsor Vacation Bible School (VBS) that kept our interest through special events in the programming. One of these was Bible Bucks. Bucks allowed us to purchase items such as book markers, crayons, pencils, and coloring books. But the granddaddy of them all was a brand new Bible, which cover could zip open and close. The cost of this precious jewel was a whopping 100 Bible Bucks, and seemingly unattainable for a poor kid. Grace sensed my desire to acquire one. She told me that it would be hard work but if I did the memory verses and brought a few friends, it could be done. I was able to bring along a few of my friends, even some I didn't really know - until I met them through trusted buddies. Grace and Andy knew them and somehow I was able to get enough Bucks to purchase the coveted prize. I began to read the Bible. Such is another human way of getting values taught and adopted in the lives of the young. I have been greatly benefited in my life from Grace and Andy and others like them. They gave me a life interest in the church. It began my lifelong interest in the church ministry for the mission of Jesus Christ.

My deep gratitude goes to this wonderful couple who gave sacrificially through prayer and deeds to insure the spiritual well-being of those who would accept their offer and care. Through the years, I often reflect on their loving attitudes and concern that accepted me in a non–judgmental orientation but at the same time encouraged me to strive for excellence including and especially the sometimes neglected matters of spiritual interests and values.

My grade school years were marked with teachers, coaches, friends and mentors who seemed to have had natural abilities to capture the potential of the little people. What's more, they made it their objective to assist youngsters to reach heights that were seemingly unattainable for children unless a team of adults would help progression. These preeminent (certainly preeminent to me) instructors and mentors made it their goal to find the deep waters that invited us to grow up find our way and become persons of worth and value to both self and others. They were the cultivators that tilled and fertilized the soil from their own minds and experience, pruned the branches. They watered the plants so to bring forth the fruit of maturity. They even pointed ways to protect the plants from invaders who would seek to neutralize or destroy the emerging person. My life had fallen into pleasant places, in a wholesome environment. I do not sense the pattern to be as strong for the very young as it was for me during those 'innocent' days.

The metaphor changes as the children grow older. They must, at last, take life on for themselves.

The nurturing, the plowing, the watering period closes. Now the imagination of the young person must take over. He or she needs a spark that will catch fire and burn brightly. That is found in the child's imagination. Imagination is the ground of creativity and when matured opens the doors to possibilities related to reality. Although I did not become a professional baseball player, the dream of becoming one did lead me along a path of understanding the formula that hard work with desire and discipline equates to success. My coaches and teachers taught me that. There has to be generated some fire in the belly. I rightly feel passionate that every child should have adults, teachers, mentors, friends, parents, who become the angels for children to turn the sparks of dreams and potential into reality and meaning. That yearning to in a child to be grown-up must be taken on in reality by each individual for self and service to society. Some children never get it, even when the growing up years are in right context.

Life sparks are to be fueled, not watered.

*Grass Valley Little League Cardinals (1967).*
*Yours truly third from right, bottom row.*

Putting Big Sticks by Little Sticks

# 3
# From Mountains to Valley

*"Ask don't steal"*
Mr. Eslinger

It is common for youngsters to accept inconveniences for home and life unless they are harassed in the context of their everyday activity. My young life was rather well adjusted in Grass Valley, despite family poverty. I lived in a home that seemed adequate even though it would not serve well for older children. I enjoyed the only family I knew intimately. We accepted each other – in love. It included two younger brothers, Mom and Dad, even if Dad was away much of the time. Mother coped with life as it was, and managed. There was a wonderful woods back of the house laced with paths for endless delight and discovery. Nature was a gift to me. I often unwrapped that gift. Parent-like friends took me to church programs and a school that challenged me in my emerging interests. Of a sudden my little world seemed about to fall apart. The "worst" thing happened. We boys were informed that the family was going to move to Oroville on the northeastern edge of the great valley that dips down the center of the State of California. We were told that our life in Grass Valley was over. Why? This was home. We could cope with daily life here and find happiness. We were mountain boys. Valleys were for sissies. There were no woods to conquer.

This home in Grass Valley was where my friends were found, where my baseball team was located, and where 'the woods' loomed up for exploration. This all seemed normal to me, and I believed I would become bereft without it. Would I find new friends? Did they have Little League? And most important were there places to investigate the world similar to those woods yonder from the backyard? Mother assured me that friends would be found and she would make sure I would be on a team. As far as exploration, she did not know, but was sure that there would be plenty of places for me to make new discoveries. She worked on my orientation knowing that it would be especially difficult for me, her oldest and most inquisitive child. She prepared me for change by accenting the new benefits, and retaining some features from the old, like Little League, in the changed venue. I was comforted. Mom had a marvelous way with her boys.

We were really moving because we were poor, and the future was going to be brighter for the family in a new assignment for Dad's employment. This true reason for the move was not emphasized to my brothers and me. It is good that a child doesn't feel poverty as the adults feel and engage it, especially in the pressure for the care and expense of growing small children. Money in our Grass Valley home became scarce as we edged farther along from the last pay day and closer to the next. In an attempt to make the few dollars stretch, Mom would cook up a big pot of beans, and if we were fortunate bits of hamburger would be added. New clothes were something of a luxury and if we did get them they were usually for me, the eldest. Of course they would be handed down consecutively to my brothers. My youngest brother, Dean, received near tattered garments well mended when Arnie and I grew out of them. My brothers and I took it all in stride and accepted it as a natural and logical solution. There was no complaint. The whole of our lives seemed to be the way life is supposed to be, and we didn't know any rich folks. Such is the attitude of youngsters if they are not overly indoctrinated about home economics. They do need to be guided to adjust to the lifestyle permitted by the resources available. We boys accepted the limitations. It was the order of life. We found our own joys in the creations of home and nature. It was a wholesome environment, and it didn't cost much in material wealth.

At the beginning of the school year each of us received a new pair of shoes and instructed to care of them. They had to last for nine months – from the beginning of school in the fall to the end of June. By the time spring came around, holes had appeared in the soles. No problem. We learned how to install cardboard every few days so to achieve the goal until bare feet time. During the summer, we would go everywhere bare-foot. It was our way even when picking black berries or hiking to the public swimming pool. Stepping on nails and pulling thorns out of the bottom of our feet was a common occurrence. That's life and kids adapt when they are accepted and loved – sometimes even when they are not.

During those early years, my brothers and I slept in the same bed. Arnie and I would lie in the same direction, with feet south, while Dean would sleep in the opposite direction with his feet north - near our torsos. To this day I remember the irritation of my coarse feet catching on the blanket or Dean's feet rubbing against me. Screams of: "You're touching me!" - would interrupt the quiet of the night. We learned to not move about while sleeping so to remain somewhat rigid in our assigned positions. Three boys had one room, one bed and took the arrangement in stride, even when it did seem crowded and inconvenient. Again – kids are flexible, even when their feet smell.

For me, the convincing argument for our move was that Dad found a house that had three bedrooms and two baths. That meant that my brothers would share a room and, since I was the eldest, I would have my own room with my own bed, free from abrasive and smelly feet. It also meant I would have my own closet and place to keep my baseball cards; my walls to display my own posters and pennants; and most important, my place to escape to my own dream about and the expanse of the world. I would roam about all of it in mental reverie. That last may have been the clincher. Waiting for a bathroom was not going to be the problem as it had been. I became a booster for the move. Bathrooms seemed better than woods. The decision was made and I felt warm to the new venture. Mom had done a good and complete persuasion job for my psyche. Moms often have a way of doing that.

Our new life style meant that we would be able to afford new clothes for my brothers and me. We would now get two pairs of shoes throughout the school year thus avoiding cardboard inserts. It also meant we would be able to enjoy finest cuisine such as spaghetti, chicken, and pork chops. The hot dogs belonged to the baseball field. We had fewer beans in the valley.

Family excitement grew with anticipation of transplanting to a larger home and a new experience. Even then, I was impacted with childhood regret that I was leaving our Grass Valley home which had meant so much to me in learning about life as it opened through the eyes and experience of a lad yearning for adventure. My father was now promoted, therefore able to earn a wage that would make life better for us. That also became a part of my learning. I was beginning to understand adult realities. Being poor didn't make much difference to the kids. It meant a great deal of concern for the grownups.

Retrieving a map I was able to determine that Oroville lay in the foothills of eastern Butte County about a half hour north of Marysville. In California travel is usually measured in time needed to get there from here. A half hour means thirty miles unless one is in a major city. I was familiar with Marysville because my dad was stationed there working on a California Division of Highways striping crew. The name was later changed to CalTrans, now quite famous in the State. His job was to paint the lines in the middle of the highway. He seemed to like his job and was proud of his position as head striper. He would often give me bits of information about the processes of striping a road and the perceptions of drivers. Drivers when traveling down the road at high speeds might be misled in their maneuvers with allusions that the lines were shorter than they actually were. They might presume they were only a few feet – so to miscalculate distances. Actually they were ten feet with breaks of twenty between them. The planning of the striping saved many dollars for taxpayers, and certainly saved many lives. Driving at night on a road without stripes may become difficult, even dangerous, especially for persons with impaired eyesight or limited skills. Good stripes offer safer driving for alert drivers. My dad was important to the modern world.

While working on the striping crew dad would often have to stay away from home for days at a time. His new job as a supervisor on a road maintenance crew was not only a promotion but it would permit him to come home virtually every night. Dad was particularly excited about the new position because it meant more money which we desperately needed and family presence. We weren't living in abject poverty but our income was less than modest. Life would be easier with our move – and it was. We all felt promoted. I was beginning to understand family economics. It is good for kids to know their parents are worthy in service to others.

A few weeks before we were to relocate, my parents took my brothers and me to visit the great Oroville Dam while it was in late stages of construction. My recollection of the trip remains with me as an adventure. I stood at an observation point, looking down in the valley, watching the trucks transporting dirt. This dam would hold back the largest man-made lake in the world.

It measured 770 feet high and over 6,900 feet long with a storage capacity of over 3.5 million acre feet. (There are seas that are smaller.) I was fascinated by the enormity of the project and felt the wonderment about how it was to be constructed. (An acre foot is the amount of water one foot deep on an acre of land). How did the workers know where to place the material and where did it come from? How were they able to hold the water back while they built the dam? The seeds sown for an unseen surveyor were germinating in my mind. It all became 'wonderful' to a lad – almost 'out of this world.' It seemed like I was growing up. I am told that we show an aptitude for learning when we ask such questions. Teaching a child to ask non-judgmental questions is a part of good parenting. It is necessary for adequate education.

Later, I learned the complexities of the project and the extensive planning that made it all work. A series of canals were constructed to divert the water to reservoirs. The cold water from winter run off was permitted to warm a bit before release for irrigation. Rice, a common crop in northern California grows better with warmer water. These canals and reservoirs also offered transport lanes for the material to construct the dam. To all this construction wizardry the State was forming a magnificent recreation area for the people that included boating, picnicking, swimming and general outdoor sports.

It was just before Christmas that we moved to our new home located on the north side of the entrance to "Copley Acres". Across the street lived Jim Bagley who was the same age as I. We immediately became best friends and he introduced me to other kids in the neighborhood. Jim and I would spend a lot of time together, especially during the summer months. With the help of his dad we built a platform tree house and a small fort in a wooded area overlooking an ephemeral creek in his backyard. His dad was one of the lead engineers in constructing the series of canals from the dam to the reservoirs. We had a first class engineer for our play house. Our move from Grass Valley was getting better all the while.

Since our move was at the school's Christmas break, my brothers and I took advantage of the opportunity to get to know our new found friends. They began quizzing us on where we were from what we did for fun. We told them during the winter we usually played in the snow. However, Oroville is situated about 300 feet above sea level and with its relatively warm climate that was rarely a snow fall. If there was a bit of snow, it would quickly melt away. This was a somewhat discouraging to my brothers and me since we were used to snow and its playful interludes of snowball fights and sledding.

My brothers and I with our new found friends got the bright idea of using the leaf from the kitchen table for dry sledding. Dry sledding is basically the same premise as sledding in snow but without the snow. The table leaf was perfect because it had wooden handles on the overhang to grip, and the top had a Formica finish. That finish was hard so to permit maximum velocity down the paved surface of our slanted driveway. The house was about 12 feet above the road and had a driveway with a rather steep incline of about 15%. The change in home domicile from Grass Valley demanded creativity for new forms of play. We possessed sufficient creativity for the purpose, even if the inventions are not acceptable for parental approval or Olympic events.

We discovered that by spreading a light layer of sand and gravel on the surface of the drive we could travel even faster – supersonic, or so it seemed. Because the driveway connected to public road and we held modest concern for our lives in the lightening like descent, we thought it best to place spotters at the lower end of the driveway to let us know if cars were approaching. On occasion the spotter wasn't alert and near misses occurred that must have caused some panic to both drivers and passengers only to subside with great relief when no accident occurred. The close calls were followed with an extended string of expletives – sent to us from drivers' windows.

After several fun filled trips we inspected the sled and discovered that the physics of abrasive gravel was wearing down the Formica top. We determined that if we had any chance of escaping punishment we had better return the make-shift luge back to its spot in the garage. We succeeded without any one discovering our project – until later. During Christmas, relatives came to our house to celebrate the Holidays and our new home. To accommodate all the guests, Dad went to the garage to retrieve the table leaf only to find the Formica was severely damaged. We escaped chastisement because of the joyful occasion and the mood was not to be spoiled by ancient history of ill-advised antics of adventuresome boys. One of the major insights helpful in theories of childhood is that it is better to be found out when there are visitors than when there are just members of the nuclear family present. With visitors there is usually laughter, even a sense of cleverness assessed for the creative gestures of kids. If there had been only the five family members present at the time of discovery, there would have been, in the younger generation, some weeping, wailing and gnashing of teeth. - generated by severe reactions from a troubled and exasperated Dad.

After the Holidays we were enrolled in different schools, my brothers went to Eastside while I was enrolled in the Bird Street School. Bird Street was founded in 1867 and was constructed as a two story Victorian style building. From 1867 to 1914 the building received several expansions and eventually formed to enclose 16 classrooms by the time I arrived in January 1968. The school had little lawn area. The surface surroundings were mostly black top. This was a bit of a shock because I was used to the grassy areas of Union Hill where I could run even dive across the surface during sporting events. On the first occasion of playing baseball, I forgot about the asphalt and dove for the ball catching it to the cheers of my classmates. However, it left a nasty scar on my hip that I have to this day. After that, my play was not with such reckless abandon. Baseball deserves grass. A school without it deserves some of the student truancy it receives. The environment of persons, young or old, should not be determined by brick, stone and macadam. There ought to be something of nature in our everyday and ordinary experiences, but especially for baseball. God gave us grass, mankind gave us macadam.

Notwithstanding my perception of suffering the trauma of not having any grass, the school had almost three times the students as Union Hill in Grass Valley. At first I felt a bit lost in the masses. However, after a few directions from some teachers I found my classroom on the second floor. The first person I met was a robust dark haired man who wore the traditional suit and black tie commonly worn during that time period. He introduced himself as Mr. Thompson and made me, the new kid, feel at ease. He showed me to my desk and gave me a subtle interview asking questions of my favorite subject and sports. As a kid I didn't realize that he was trying to find out how far along I might be found in education. For the remainder of the year he took special interest in me. I responded, and found out later that he recommended that upon entering the 7th grade that I be placed in the enrichment program for students who demonstrated potential which is for students that they believe may have demonstrated abilities to excel.

Shortly after I began at Bird Street a marble craze took place that lasted several weeks. Different types of marbles were being brought to school and competition arose. Who had the best marbles? Were they real agates or glass? Shooting galleries were constructed to lure students to put their prized marbles on the block. These galleries consisted of several styles and each with a differing enticement. The two basic ones were the circle and the pit. A circle was drawn in the dirt around the reward while the pit was simply a hole in the ground. A distance from the treasure would be determined. The customer would then roll his marble towards it and if the missile fell in the pit or circle, the young shooter would win whatever was in it. If he missed, the gallery owner would keep the marble. The diameter and distance would always be dependent upon the quality of the marble or marbles. From this we learned commerce and trade. However, school administrators viewed it as gambling and the enthusiasm soon faded away. My Las Vegas recess was shortly over. I would have to work for a living. I never lost my marbles.

It was at this school that I found friends that became integral to my daily life. They helped me obtain contact information for Little League. Mom signed me up and I was picked to play for the Orioles. Our team came in near the bottom of the league that year winning only three or four games. However, I got to play every game and was one of their top players at shortstop. No longer did I look for walks but instead I learned how to deliver timely hits and field balls when they were hit to me. I no longer was a support player but became a leader for the team. I was growing up, and learning my favorite physical activity that held life lessons for me. My dreams were being realized, and the effective participation gave me physical confidence. I wasn't just a little kid anymore. The context of sports served me well.

Not only was I growing physically but I also increased in awareness of my spiritual life interests along the way. About a year before we left Grass Valley, my Mom started attending the Nazarene Church with us. Grace and Andy told us about a Nazarene Church in Oroville and suggested we go there. During my first week at Bird Street one of my classmates, Don Libby, told me that he went to the church and would meet me there on Sunday. I told Mom and she took us to the church – new to us, but not for long. The church people immediately embraced us and we felt at home much the same way as we did in Grass Valley. We were fitting in well with our new environment. Life seemed to be orderly, and getting better all the while – great for kids.

With school out for summer and Little League over, my brothers and I searched for ways to overcome boredom. Venturing out in the neighborhood we sought our friends to assist in expanding mutual creativity for new adventures.

In the back yard of our home about 50 feet apart with a gentle slope between them were two oak trees. To this day I am not sure what gave us, the venturesome lads, the idea, but it was probably an adventure movie of some sort – agreed upon to act out in some way. We found a pulley in the garage and one of our friends brought a rope. We tied the rope to one tree, inserted the pulley and tied the other end to the second tree. We ran the pulley up to the higher tree and one of the neighbor lads rode it down only to be crushed against the lower tree. When he regained consciousness, we checked out his wounds, and determined to modify the ride somewhat. Our solution was to remove a mattress from Dean's bed, since he was the youngest (the most easily influenced for the good of the order), and tie it to the lower tree thus softening the arrival of the lad still elevated in space at the close of the ride. It worked to perfection! It was a bit hard on the mattress.

After numerous trips down the rope coupled with excitement and laughter, we came to the reality that Mom and Dad might not approve of Dean's mattress being used as a buffer. It was beginning to show some degree of unexpected wear. Struck with a need for caution we ended the Disney-like ride for the day and successfully snuck it back to Dean's bed. All turned out well for our venture and would remain a mystery except that in adulthood, Dean now complains of a bad back caused by sleeping on a lumpy mattress. If challenged for my part in a creative enterprise, I would demand an authoritative opinion about the cause of an unanticipated accident. It wasn't my fault – was it?

With all this Huck Finn and Tom Sawyer activity I was beginning to sense ideas related to right and wrong. One event made a deep impression on me. Behind the house and beyond the oak trees was an orchard. I don't recall with certainty the species of trees in the orchard but if I remember correctly it was a grove of walnut trees, a common crop in Northern California. I was not particularly fond of walnuts but I loved Thompson seedless grapes. Mr. Eslinger lived behind us and was the owner and guardian of a handsome crop of the coveted prize – Thompson Grapes. One day my brothers and several neighbor lads decided they wanted to climb the fence, six feet high, that bordered the property line and make a foray that would rescue a few grape clusters. For some reason I had a twinge of moral response and decided not to participate any further in these clandestine activities. The young thieves, my brothers and friends, told me in advance that I would not share in the spoils. I accepted the judgment rather than be shamed into participation. It seemed fair enough. I refused to lead or participate in this one. I had a tinge of self-righteousness.

I stayed around to observe the venture. It wasn't long until I witnessed acts that defied the laws of nature. Racing through the orchard and returning to our back yard at a pace that would be the envy of the Jesse Owens, my former colleagues hurtled the six foot high barbed wire fence in Olympic form. Only a few strides behind them, was Mr. Eslinger, who thought better of attempting the same maneuver of the fence line, stopping just short the fence. He stood for a few moments until a broad smile came across his face as he watched the athletic thieves descend over the cut bank and out of view.

He noticed me as a spectator and asked if I knew these recalcitrant displaying super physical abilities. At that moment I was so stunned by what I had just witnessed that it left me speechless. I shrugged as though uncertain.

Recognizing my disability to 'rat' on my generation, he instructed me "Tell them that if they want some grapes come ask me, don't steal from me."

A few days later, I told the perpetrators what Mr. Eslinger had said and asked them if they wanted to go with me to ask for grapes. They quickly responded: "No way! He's mean!" I decided to go anyway. They were all amazed that he gave me a big brown paper bag full of the sweet fruit. It was shared with all. (Righteousness does payoff.) I felt good about learning something of values, and not to assume that someone is mean because he did not approve of stealing grapes. The feeling of some virtue swept over me. It did teach me something of values. I don't want to get over the lesson. By sharing with the guys I was returning good for evil. They had not shared with me, and I had not stolen grapes. Boy – were those Thompson grapes goood! They were devoutly consumed.

Even so I knew I had a long way to go in this growing-up business. I remain astonished that we did not have serious accidents in some of the escapades. On the west side of our house was a soft fill bank. One day we decided to take our little green army men and play war maneuvers at that location. Small tanks, jeeps and trucks were pulled into the battle while sounds of bombs and shooting saturated the battle field. In an effort to better simulate realism, gasoline was retrieved from the garage along with matches. The fuel was sprinkled on the ground and on a few of the toys. Matches served as missiles to launch the attack. We were clearly winning a battle against a fierce imaginary foe. We had the right weapons.

During the course of battle the ammo dump was hit but so was the small gasoline can. In something of a panic, one of the soldiers threw the can which struck and ignited a nearby oak tree. To our relief the spectacle only lasted a few moments and quickly subsided leaving the tree blackened along one side. All were sworn to secrecy and a vow was contracted that we would say nothing to anyone, even if we faced torture. We were lads of integrity with each other.

A few days later my father returned from work assignments, stood in the driveway and stared quizzically at the blackened oak. He reflected out loud: "Why is that tree black and with no leaves?" My response was to give a token gaze at the odd scene and shrug my shoulders. (The gesture had served me well with Mr. Eslinger on the grape stealing episode, and it worked here.) I am grateful trees have no vocal cords. He glanced at me, then back at the tree, and then mumbled something about the tree probably dying. With that he went into the house. No more was spoken of the incident until we finally confessed to the crime some years later, well after the spanking age of parent to child. That was the easy way out. I have learned that if you can't have guests for dinner and gain absolution through that means, wait for adulthood when you can laugh and get forgiveness in sharing memories. If only it were that easy for the really serious stuff in life. (I learned later that a wife doesn't take the shrug as a gesture of ignorance or innocence.)

Those were fun - filled days at Copley Acres and Bird Street School. I look back at in memories, good and ill, of boyhood shenanigans and serious involvements that were filled with valuable lessons. Through all of it I adjusted to my surroundings and found friendship and adventure outside of Grass Valley. The world was growing larger.

But there was another boyhood experience, very large in the incorporation of events, and the changed environment of the valley that also contributed

to my emerging life, personality and direction. It was an incident that would forever change our family and caused us to seek the deep waters within us that cry for faith and understanding, which eventually led to invaluable insight of the multifaceted meaning of responsibility, flexibility, and determination to never give up. That review belongs to my next chapter.

*My brothers, Jim Bagley, and myself built a fort on the creek across from our home in Copley Acres. We took it seriously in defending our fort as demonstrated by my brother Don (Dean).*

# 4
# Lady Bugs and Mom

*"Let her shout!"*
*Dad*

My first childhood recollection of Mom is that she had always been present with no defining moment of introduction. For me, there is no distinct flash in time where it suddenly occurred to me that she existed. She was just always there. If I needed something to eat, she would supply the need. If I needed somebody to treat my scratches and scrapes; there she was with a Band Aide and Bactine. When I was congested she would apply Vick's Vapor Rub to my chest. I don't know if it worked but I know I would have rather suffered from the cold than to have that stuff' on my chest. My objections fell on Mom's seemingly deaf ears. Her cheering assurances won the day. I knew I would recover. There was always the victory of Mom.

On one occasion while playing with other children on an old abandoned car, I slipped and fell onto a stump bruising my tailbone. Rolling on the ground and crying from the excruciating pain my mother came bolting out of the house to rescue her child. Sweeping me in her arms she comforted me. She placed me carefully in a prone position in the back seat of the car, pushed my brothers in the front seat and sped to the doctor's office. She suffered the embarrassment of my oversight in the absence of my underwear. She told me a rule that too this day I obey: Always have underwear on and make sure it's clean. It became one of thousands of Mom's commandments. I keep most of them to this day – never failing in the underwear commandment. I still think the main purpose should have focused on my bruised body. Instead it was underwear.

When Dad got paid; my brothers and I would pile in the car and she would drive into a parking slot of an A&W Root Beer stand. The attendant would come out and Mom would order Baby Burgers and frosty mugs of root beer for her three boys. If she had enough money, she would order the Momma burger. All the while I would pester her to order me the Teen Burger. I remember the day she weakened and ordered it for me. Those times seemed special because

We were being treated by our Mom. There was a pleasant mystery in the event. They didn't just seem special – they were special. Every kid should have that kind of experience – repeated as often as circumstances permit, but in some mysterious way seem memorable for families. At least the teen burger was invested with the miracle of Mom. So beautiful is the memory of it all, I must write about it. Savor it with me.

When I was eight years of age she signed me up to play baseball. She would make sure I was at all the practices, and at every game, even though it didn't take prompting from anyone to get me there. She was with me all the way. It was there that I learned team work and sportsmanship. She also enrolled us into Cub Scouts where I made it to the rank of We Belo gaining good concepts of moral character and learning value belonging to life. I may not have understood life, but I was living it. With the aid of a dear friend Mom made sure that we attended church regularly. It was there that I learned that I not only had a physical body but also had a soul to give and relate to Christ. I submitted to Christ as a lad. It was the best decision I ever made. I was given appreciation for spiritual and material life – a gift to wholeness of being. Mom provided those constructive life avenues for me. The older I become, the more deeply do I appreciate the values and life context Mom worked on for her boys. She yearned for the same values and context for her man, husband and my Dad. He was a man of the world.

Dad's interests were rather earthy and casual which is often the way of it in modern families.

My Dad did not attend the church in Grass Valley nor did he have any desire to go to the church in Oroville. Dad felt at the time that the church was not for him. He had a propensity to stop off at the local tavern for a beer or two with some friends before coming home. For him, attending a church on Sunday and go to a drinking establishment on Friday would be hypocrisy.

I understand the honesty, but my youthful concerns for all of life nagged at me. Some values and conducts clashed. I remember one day Andy, who took my brothers and I to church, encouraged him to come along with us. Dad's response was that if he attended church, it would burn down. The next Sunday he did go and the following day the second floor caught fire. You can imagine what he made of that. It struck us in the telling. It seemed like he was either a prophet, or a setter of fires. It may be that God was challenging him.

Despite my father's misgivings about his own attendance at church he adamantly encouraged us to go. We quickly found friends there that accepted us graciously. The congregation was a strong family oriented group that loved people where they found them regardless of their background. They understood our situation with the reluctance of my Dad and sought ways to include him into various functions. In addition to the usual picnics, boating, and progressive dinners, they also had two softball teams, one for the women and the other for the men. This was my meat. It was a feature attractive to Dad.

Mom was an athlete in high school before she quit school at the age of 16 to marry my Dad who was 21 at the time. She loved to play softball and was easily enticed to participate on the Church team. The team did reasonably well in competition and Mom was among the top players on the team. Dad also had good athletic skills. However, he played for a local tavern, (The Shamrock) – obviously not for the church. That first year the Nazarene Church played against The Shamrock several times. The pitcher for the church happened to be the father of my good friend and classmate, Don Libby; while the pitcher for the tavern was one of Dad's good friends. They were the top two pitchers in the league and the games were very competitive. My loyalties were divided as to who I wanted to win. My friends were at the church; while my father played with people I didn't know very well. It was funny feeling I didn't like. I had a feeling of some disloyalty to somebody. It took something out of winning.

However, the following year, Dad was enticed to play for the church. This brought great relief in that my undivided allegiance was to one team. Also, there was the possibility that he would begin attending church. I wanted our whole family together in everything. That togetherness, I have discovered, is a part of effective parenting. It contributes to family life. Many families have broken up simply because they never acculturated togetherness as a value for them.

As a young lad, I was impressed with the family unity of this church and how the members interacted with each other. I yearned for our family to have the same sense of unity in our involvement with newly found friends. I wasn't old enough to make it an issue in Grass Valley. Now it was important to me. I was growing up, and wanted to gain some of the values I was learning about. My dad did not have the same desire but instead chose to socialize with his bar buddies and be acquainted with the church. The split interest had some meaning negative for the family. There was a continuing sense of division within our family. We seemed hypocritical.

In 1969, the Fourth of July fell on Friday which introduced a three day weekend. So our family planned a camping trip for the holidays with some of Dad's friends in Taylorsville. Taylorsville is a small mountain community in the Sierra Nevada mountain range about 80 miles Northeast of Oroville. That morning Mom drove my brothers and me up Highway 70 through the canyon of the North Fork of the Feather River to the campsite. Mom was assigned to drive the family car with the camping equipment and Dad would lead on his motorcycle. He had left the house earlier, for some foray. We were used to that procedure. As he had often done, Dad lingered with his buddies at a bar. Mom, with her boys, went on to the campsite without Dad's accompaniment. Mom worked around her disappointments.

We arrived at the campsite around noon and waited for Dad. He had promised to be there to cook steaks for everyone. However, he did not appear until well after the sun had set and we all had eaten. Mom was upset about his late arrival and the fact that he had obviously consumed too much beer. In an effort to reconcile differences over the matter, he talked Mom into going for a ride on the motorcycle. Mom instructed me to go to bed before she left to ride with Dad. My brothers would follow my lead. Obligingly, I rolled out the sleeping bag and went to sleep with a surreal feeling that something was not going right. The holidays were getting off to a shaky start. We boys felt something but didn't understand what it was.

The next morning as I awoke, I was surprised to find several adults sitting about in solemn silence. Sensing something was wrong, I asked for my parents. One of the adults, Pat Riddle, who owned The Shamrock, informed my brothers and me that there had been an accident, and that they would be driving us back to Oroville. We packed quickly and were on our way.

I don't remember the trip back to Oroville, but I do remember the stunning feelings about the mystery of my parents. I remember staying with the Riddle's for a few days until Dad's sister, Aunt Marie, arrived to take us home. For a lad, 13 years of age, the situation was a driving concern but I knew I had to follow the directions of the adults. They may not have managed matters well in this instance – for a teenager. During the period of a few days no one spoke of the accident. I and my brothers were in limbo - nothing. Nothing was clarified to us. It wasn't until I read an article in the local newspaper that I understood what happened and the seriousness of the situation. The article spoke of my father, "being stable," while my mother was in, "critical condition." What did this all mean? The situation seemed intolerable.

The news story was about a tragic motorcycle accident, causing near death for the cyclists. At the moment of my reading one person, my Mom, might yet die. The moment was traumatic.

A day after I discovered the story we boys were taken to visit my father in recovery from a broken leg and torn artery in his right forearm. There were other scrapes and bruises, painful but not serious. From his hospital bed he explained to us that we needed to wait to see Mom until he was released. During our visit with him there was a sense given to me about him – which he had changed. He seemed more 'grown up!' The accident got his attention to something. We had not seen him in this mood and serious mien before. The look in his eye was calmness and peace that made me feel better, even lifted so to believe that all would be well. Whatever went wrong there would be recovery. What a relief for me and my brothers.

The day I was permitted to see her in the hospital my brothers and I stood outside the hospital as Dad debriefed us on the magnitude of her injuries. He seemed unconcerned about his own situation as he stood with the aid of crutches and a cast on his right leg. The cast extended half way up the thigh. There was a firm gauze bandage wrapped around his right arm covering the artery repairs. He said: "She hit her head and broke her leg in the accident. She's pretty bruised up and doesn't look the same as you remember her. She will recover. She will be ok. So whatever you feel, you do not cry. You don't want to upset her."

Because I was the eldest son I was the first to go while my brothers waited outside with Aunt Marie. As Dad led me down the hallway, an experience I well remember, there was a solemn silence except for the methodical suctioning sound of his crutches against the floor creating evidence of seriousness. I never felt like this before. We would make it through. I determined to keep my emotions in check and to be strong for Mom. The room was brightly illuminated. Mom was prone on the hospital bed, slightly on her right side with her back toward me. I circled the foot of her bed and as I came face to face I realized that Dad could not have prepared me for what a loving son would see in his mother so physically broken. Her head was grotesquely swollen and bruised. Several of her teeth were missing. Her hair from her head had been entirely shaved so the doctors could drill several opening through the skull bone to relieve the pressure of blood accumulating on her brain. I realized in that few moments that life would never be the same for our family. From this point everything would not be new or repeated from pleasant habit – but different. I felt overwhelmed with what I saw and felt, but remembered the firm words of my father in facing any moments of despair. I was able to hold back the tears pressing my eyes. I forced out a meek and choking: "Hi Mom." She then opened the eye that was not completely swollen shut and affectionately gazed at me. There was love, and I knew it – and felt it. What a moment! It lives within me.

Realizing her unbroken leg was exposed, she attempted to cover it with the white hospital sheet – even in her condition, I had a serendipitous experience. Here was my Mom, and she was going to make it. Before that meeting I heard the whispers that they didn't think she was going to survive. If she did, they thought and gave their words to it, that she would live the rest of life with severe brain damage. Her cognitive skills would be virtually non-existent. However, at those first moments with me, she had the awareness to understand her motherly modesty example to her children. She was still Mom in thought and action, indicating to me the normality of her thinking so that I should not despair for this horrendous accident. For a moment as I looked into her good and loving eye, I saw into the recesses of her soul and found a determination to overcome whatever adversities would follow. She was communicating to me that she trusted her family in assisting her to recovery. There was no complaint. The path ahead was not one of fear and sorrow but rather a trail to be explored that would ultimately lead to new discoveries. However, the route proved to be arduous. It eventually would lead to triumph. The athletic woman was gone, but my Mom was going to be with us. I felt full Thanksgiving.

There was an unspoken resolve that emanated from Dad that he was going to take on the responsibility to lead our family through and out of this tragedy. His calm action generated from more than sorrow for his wife's dire situation - which he had caused. He seemed to have suddenly received a divine calling. As he lay bleeding on the paved road, at the time of the accident and unable to assist mother who was unconscious and mangled several yards away, he called upon his Creator for intervention in the tragedy. He deeply felt his depravity and resolved that he would no longer be aloof to family matters if God would help in this horrible event and save the life of his wife. He bargained with God for Mom's life. His own future may have been included in the bargaining.

The first Sunday after he was released from the hospital he awakened me and my brothers with instructions to get ready for church. We readied ourselves while Dad dressed up better than usual for Sunday. Our thoughts, as we drove to the church, were that he would do the usual and drop us off, then continue on to the local tavern. Even so, something seemed different. Instead of pulling up to the curb to let us out, he pulled into the parking lot and turned off the motor. My brothers and I looked on in disbelief as he wrestled with new crutches to steady himself outside the car. With warmth, we were a bit animated in the realization he was going to attend with us. We were family, and in the right place.

During the service, I sat next to him in something of a daze at the shift of everything. Mom wasn't there, Dad was. As the service was ending Dad, with the help of his crutches, rose to his feet and pressed his way down the aisle to the low lying alter in the front. There he laid the crutches down and attempted to maneuver himself into a kneeling position. Immediately he was engulfed by loving members of the church as he, on his own, dedicated his life to a new beginning. It took some doing – some humbling of spirit. I knew it was real. We boys were with him, and he was with us. He was to be our new Dad.

With a support group in place for prayer and assistance from the Church people, Dad enlisted my brothers and me for help in Mom's recovery. For the next six months we worked with her every day to try to bring her back to being Mom again in fact as well as in spirit. She could not feed herself, so we had to feed her much like feeding an infant. She could not walk so we had to physically help her stand and hold her up to strengthen her legs and to help her recover motor skills. She could not speak so we had tried to help her form words. Skeptics did not believe it would be possible to take her home. They did not know the depth of faith held by Mom and Dad and their three sons. That faith prevailed.

There are experiences in life when we gain connection with fellow human beings where there are no symbols or melodies that can capture the elevating life of love and connection. It is a flash that is felt and comes from the deep wells of our being. It then grows practically, even spiritually. It grips our lives and endears us to be willing captives of each other. These are moments we want to revisit the memory banks of our minds. They make us better persons. They show us we belong to each other in some elevated standing. They serve us and others.

One day as I was sitting outside Mom's room at the convalescent hospital, on a sudden I heard Mom shouting in a slow labored cadence "I... l o v e ...y o u! I... l o v e ...t h e.... b o ys!" There was excitement in her voice as she repeated the words over and over; each time louder than the last. She was speaking for the first time since the accident. Dad was grinning from ear to ear. The silence was over. Love had restored her voice.

"Dad, isn't she a little loud?" I said. "Let her shout." he replied.

And she did shout with everything she had "I love you! I love the boys!" What a celebration! The moment was and remains above and beyond words. There was something spiritual in it, and it remains in my memory. Love. For a few moments nothing else occurred in the world.

It seemed I was learning an angel sing. It was a moment in time that cemented an immortal connection within our family. We were willing to embrace the realization of the miracle before us. The scene was imprinted into the memory of our lives that we were, thereafter, eager to recall. It was a soul imprint that made us understand a mother's love and a father's determination. It held forever in it.

Like the ladybugs in the forest when as a small lad I thought I had a special discovery – a secret of my own, I now gained it in an infinitely higher sense with human beings. I felt God had entrusted me with seeing the heart of a mother and father holding genuine love. Looking back at that moment, I came to the realization I had discovered the origin of a true parent's heart. She was fighting for her life to be the way it was, to be Mom again. For the rest of her life her ambition, her goal, her desire was to be a wife to my father and our Mom. My father's wrongs were to be forgiven and absolved. My parents succeeded in all. The whole of it was to teach three boys, and anyone looking in, where life's values are to be found in experience. We emerged with victorious encounter even while wondering: Why did this happen to us? The tunnels of life seem to make the light brighter on the other side of the tunnels. Our Mom and Dad survived to be Mom and Dad again, and at a level higher than when they were physically whole.

Mom and Dad were deeply concerned about our welfare even after my brothers and I grew to adulthood. They prayed for our marriages, our jobs, and our lives. One time while I was in the hospital with an infection and a temperature nearing 105°; my mother put her face inches away from mine and told me: "You better get better!" I had to. I knew that if I did not, I would have to suffer her loving wrath… so I got better. It can be done you know. We proved it.

My brothers and I were always known to them as their "boys." They embraced our wives and our children. They wanted what we wanted. They were quick to forgive and always prepared to offer their last dollar if they thought we needed it.

The years have slipped by into decades, and a new millennium launched. A memory for me recent in the period of my review for writing a memorial of them, involved my parents and I attending spring training baseball games. We chatted about a number of things, ate hot dogs and drank sodas. They loved to watch baseball which was one of the interests we intently shared in common in our family. I was blessed to have a Mom and Dad like them. They made ordinary life special for their boys. There is a forever feeling about it.

On July 10, 2012 a little after 5pm, Dad informed me that like the lady bugs I had lost as a little guy, that: "Mom is gone." Questions filled my mind, higher but similar to the disappearance of the lady bugs and my responsibilities related to some divine information. Where did she go? Is she alright? Had I fulfilled the responsibilities entrusted to me from the divine Master in learning from the love of Mom's heart? Did she know how much I loved her and appreciated all the sacrifices she made? All I could do was express my concern to my heavenly Father. Like my Mom He was not scolding but assuring and healing my sense of loss. It is lament, not grief. He informs me in Scripture that Mom is a citizen of His Kingdom. She is made whole again, no longer in danger and moved on to a better context than earth provides. I assume she has been rescued from marauding boys and dogs.

The Apostle Paul visited Mars Hill in Athens, Greece where learned and scholarly men assembled to seek the answers to the great questions of life. Paul informed them, as recorded in

Acts 17:27; "'So that they should seek the Lord, in the hope that they might grope for Him and find Him, though He is not far from each one of us." These words comfort me in that even though I grope for the answers, if I seek the Lord, He is not far from me and will be found. Mom is with God; therefore, Mom is not far from me. In that faith we, in our family, find closure, and a raft of beautiful memories of a loving heart.

Is there an angel in the kingdom of God who could drop a note from me? It reads: "Mom, thank you for entrusting me with your heart and being my Mom. I love you, forever."

With it I send another very short appreciation note of prayer to our forever Friend: "Thanks, God."

*On our way to see Sutter's Mill in Coloma, California where gold was first discovered and set off the Gold Rush of 1849. My mom is leading the way while holding Dean. Following are Arnie and myself.*

Putting Big Sticks by Little Sticks

# 5
# *The Accidental Family*

*"Hit it with a rock!"*
Kirk Göhre

Families commonly compose and use expressions or phrases growing out of discernible family events – both pleasant and unpleasant. When the adapted phrases are used, family members and close friends understand the meaning in mutual agreement. No further explanation is necessary. It may be a large meaning like: "before the war" or "after the depression." It is commonly used in even larger exchange: "Where were you when you heard President Kennedy was shot?" Or "What were you doing on 9-11?" It may be something personal applying only to one family. It represents an experience or feeling growing out of experience, good or ill, likely stemming from a shared episode that may lead to bonding feelings for inclusive persons. For our family 'The Accident' described not only the exact time period the incident occurred but it also labeled and pointed to suffering, directed to change and recovery from tragedy for our family. The Accident of course was the motorcycle event that nearly ended the lives of my parents.

The 'Accident' became a benchmark of understanding for everything that followed for Mom, Dad, and their sons. It ultimately proved to each of us that adversity can be overcome with faith, forgiveness, determination and hard work to make better persons of us than we might have become in improved circumstances. We learned that faith is not only in God, but in each of us relating to each other. Trust ensues. Faith is not external but internal affecting external experience. It becomes a possession of trust that has become external in conduct and the way we think and live. We trust those in whom we have faith. Oftentimes when trouble or confusion arose we would go back to the motivating source, the 'Accident,' that we knew became an awakening to some realities and truths to guide us through problems and duties that made better persons of us. We had survived the worst that could happen to our family. The 'Accident' did that for me, and for our family members in their own assimilations. It became the standard to go back to when life seemed confusing and I needed to check the datum for accuracy and response. As noted before, the 'Accident' changed us for better persons – even for some others with whom we related.

The 'Accident,' was the near death of my father and mother in a motorcycle accident when my father, a bit 'hung over', crashed on a mountain road. He and Mother were thrown some distance from the cycle. God's sparing of their lives may be the greatest miracle of my day by day life experience. Our family believed it certainly was divinely attended. There is no other explanation for this survival-at least for us. There is too much in the context of the event to explain it in natural terms. That is the 'take' on it by our family. It is cemented in our souls and psyche.

My parents taught me by example that determination would bring us through any problem that came our way. A problem was turned into a bump in the road – to be negotiated. Events even as severe as this life threatening event were not times to despair or retreat, but occasions to rise above ordinary life and find opportunities to overcome negatives, so to move forward. They provide periods for redirection, facing new questions, and finding fresh answers - then we must follow them wherever they lead. We must not be slothful or blame others – especially each other. It was a 'roll up your sleeves' period for us, so to stimulate an overcoming attitude. Even in tragedy this attitude and belief works – if chosen and used for good. It proved so with our family. It taught me to grow up, and keep a life balance.

The Accident was a call to embrace some uncertainty in our future life journey. Although Mom never fully recovered in physical balance or athletic activity she had known, and Dad had moments when he lapsed on occasion in his personal context for life, we learned and accepted that perfection is not attainable on the earthly sojourn. We adapted and found our way to improve as persons and as a family. Together, we were family, looking to the challenge of improved approaches workable for us. In sincerity of heart we tried to put into action what we were capable of doing. It had to be done in love to succeed. So it was that we accepted each other, and worked together in the repetitious situations caused by 'the Accident.' Cooperation at more than standard levels became the norm in our lives. It helped to form us – form us into mature persons we were meant to be. So it was that tragedy turned to blessing. Even so, each member of the family made the adaptive choices, and at different intensities. Tragedy became motivation to family solidarity, appreciation and respect.

The "Accident" occurred during summer recess between the 7th and 8th grade for me, the eldest of three brothers. I adjusted my life to duty but also to do what I had always done - even in the changed family context. No matter what the circumstances, I wanted to find my way to some achievement that would meet a desire for ideals in my life. I was pushed toward maturity. That too was good for me.

I attended Central Middle School. The building was designed into four corridors and six classrooms along each corridor; two corridors for the 7th and two for the 8th. During each period all the students in one classroom would stay together and go to a different classroom on the same corridor where we were taught varied subjects. The pattern was efficient and focused, providing variety. It reduced boredom, so easy a habit for youngsters. To have a different teacher during each period specializing in another area of learning helped to stimulate us. The variety seemed to make better students. Subject matter and individual students received more attention than that found in the more casual one room school. We seemed to be more 'grown up.' The one room school was in its last days after World War II. Even so, in remote parts of the United States it survives, and does work for its communities – what with modern aides for caring teachers. Given the limitations, the education is excellent.

Middle School years address an awkward period in evolving lives - mine included. The period is sometimes dubbed as coming of age. Middle School students emerge from 'kids' to 'young people.' Emerging children may feel the process will go on interminably when in reality it lasts only two or three years, but for some the transition years are extended. The process slows for the disinterested. It takes some doing to grow up. It takes caring and wise adults in a good system to get children through life and mind transitions. During this period it seems as if it is the worst of times when in reality it may be, or become the best of times. (It seems appropriate that we read, as a required assignment the "Tale of Two Cities" with its well-known opening lines about "the best and worst of times.") We were learning what is 'up and down,' and beginning to practice 'in and out' or, 'this or that.' This is a critical age relating to choosing or evading, even shifting directions for one's life. Whispers of inclination press the emerging consciousness to take this or that foray in life. It is a serious time and many young persons are not offered assistance in the transition. Strong attitudes are formed – some affirmative, others negative.

Society often appears neutral about the matter. All this appears in the context of emerging puberty. For me I was gaining a magnificent gift – love of reading.

During my 7th grade year and before the Accident, I had the privilege of having Mr. Hixon for my home room teacher. I don't remember the specific subject he taught but I do remember him as a self-assured grey-haired man who registered deep interest in his students – to their advantage. His appearance was like that of a caring grandfather figure and his involvement with students proved the perception. We students felt we wanted something this man conveyed in his personal model to students. I sensed the concept of a model for life from him. Modeling life is a major matter for children to find life style and direction. A pattern is offered for one to accept or reject. We are sometimes measured by the models we follow. It begins for children with their parents and other family members. Soon, the community and its context offer others for guidance and courage, others for youthful carnality and rebellion. Teachers in the 'growing up' period of youngsters ought to sense a degree of parenting in imparting information, but also the persons students would like to be like – even emulate. Choices must be made. Too little is done at this stage to form the lives of emerging children. The

'Accident' forced me to serious context early in my life, and I can say that I'm grateful for those lessons. I owe compliments to many persons who now seem like they were mentors to me.

My first few days in school that year, I had some new dress shoes that were a bit too snug on my feet – so much so that blisters developed on my smallest toes. They quickly became infected. The pain became sufficiently intense that I avoided walking when I could. I even absented some days at school. Mr. Hixon called my home one day to inquire about the situation. I was too embarrassed to admit openly the reason for my absence. I generalized stating that I was not feeling well. This caused him to send me to the nurse the next day I attended school. She proclaimed me to be healthy and in fine shape, except for "sore feet." The interest of the teachers, in addition to Mr. Hixson, and none offering harsh responses made a better person of me and more respectful of caring persons. I felt I wanted to live up to the respect they gave me. I was expected to do my duty, solve my problems, and 'get on with life.' With their gracious prodding I did. My life was being guided by caring and involved professional adults – something important to the individual, the family, and society.

The reason I did not want to confess to the blisters was because of an embarrassing disclosure I would have to make. Even though our move to Oroville brought a promotion and more income, we were still at modest economic status. We could afford to purchase new clothes for Arnie and Dean instead of moving them on with 'hand-me-downs.' However, we were told at the beginning of school that the new clothes had to last throughout the school year including the new shoes. It was an annual bit of instruction that we knew from years past. Realizing that replacements were not an option because of finances, I did not feel that I could make a request for another fitting. The parental warning had achieved its purpose. I respected their decisions. It was a different, sometimes trying, period for me in efforts to please so many adults I cared about.

Before the 'Accident,' my father was indifferent to planning the welfare of his family; therefore, neither Mom nor I felt we could ask for new ones after having been warned of limitations not open to negotiation. So I dealt with it as best I could until Mom applied small bandages and treated the wounds. Admitting that the shoes were the problem meant the only remedy would be to purchase new ones, thus gaining an aloof admission from my father that something else would have to be sacrificed from the family needs. I was unprepared to receive these chilly and grousing responses.

Eventually Mother was able to finagle funds from Father to purchase tennis shoes. Even though they weren't the stylish Chuck Taylor Converse version, popular in those days, they were a welcome relief from the shoes that seemed to be designed for the infamous Lotus Feet in China. The 'foot – binding' experience of those shoes remain with me to this day – with some mysterious influence related to child rebellion.

Before I entered Central, Mr. Thompson from the Bird Street School recommended that I be included in the Enrichment Program. I was aware that I was placed with sharp students who were affluent and knowledgeable - which made me self-conscious. That self-degradation emerged long after my earlier acceptance with our family's lowly financial situation. Youngsters tend to accept each other, not thinking of contrasts and comparisons. Parents of the kids in the Enrichment Program were clearly involved with their families and provided their children with necessary materials to perform well. My situation during the years before the 'Accident' did not have an engaging father nor did we have adequate affluence. The matter of lack of affluence became more obvious to me as the years unfolded. I began to 'feel' poor and less than adequate around my peers. Feeling poor is a troublesome influence compounding the problem of actually being poor. It is a double 'whammy.' Young people are blest when someone lifts them from such awful negatives with a gift of hope. Money certainly can't buy happiness, but it does help it along. In a growing mind the negatives and affirmatives often remain to haunt or bless later memories. Studies show that the better memories usually prevail, but not always.

However, the negative youthful depressions declined for me in the summer of 1969 and the Accident, I moved along with more confidence into the 8th grade year. I sensed that I had to grow up. We boys had to shoulder part of the adults' load with our changed family context. The first year or so after the Accident, Mom and Dad were invited to several churches to share their story of the Accident. The two of them had become symbols of meaningful recovery: Mom from the physical afflictions imposed from the Accident, and Dad from the habits of human depravity. Congregations were encouraged to glimpse into greater understanding of life's purpose so to seek meaning and truth; to not be afraid to search for that meaning; and to gain courage, accepting answers not all of which may be pleasant. Their messages were testimonies of forgiveness and acceptance, the biblical approach to life and persons in experience. I was introduced to lay ministry and my part in a loving family context. We had to model what we asked of others to believe and practice. The witness of my parents relating to the Accident helped me to adapt to the new pattern. Each of us became better in conduct even to each other – in love.

Dad emerged from the accident and accepted the witness of its meaning to him. He became seriously involved in the church, and encouraged us to do the same. That was an easy request to accommodate since many of my friends attended that church. The church seemed like family. We were there for Sunday school, worship service, evening service and Wednesday night Bible studies and prayer services. No one felt coerced or obligated but rather looked forward to it as part of life. Further to its redemptive meaning the church is a society for interpersonal relationships based on love and acceptance. There was strong mutuality for the family. It was an effective way to form young lives in faith and values. We didn't rebel, and I am grateful for the balanced life. It has been what it ought to have been. I learned that there was no accident in the 'Accident' that changed our family context. Spiritual perceptions offer a difference in life forming.

Father was home more after the 'Accident' and accepted responsibilities formerly overlooked. His daily presence answered the prayers of our family for 'togetherness.' We became more serious about family meaning. Money was budgeted and saved rather than frittered away. We were doing better in life management. Dad was 'there' for Mom and their three sons, affectionately known as 'our boys.' It brought light to us from darkness, even from moments of despair, of a horrible event – the 'Accident.' Blessing may jump out of tragedy. It did for us. We learned to turn tragedy to blessing.

We learned life was not a child's concoction of what ought to be. Light may become brighter because of a darkness experience.

Soon after the 'Accident' we moved from the rented house in Copley Acres. We now owned (paying for) our own home on Las Plumas Avenue across the street from Oakdale Heights Elementary School. Mom continued in a recovery mode. Her memory worked to 'catch up.' On occasion in the early months of her recovery she thought of her boys as toddlers. We understood, but worked on her to be recognized as growing up and becoming responsible. On one occasion, we were playing baseball across the street at the school when Mom came out the door and began shouting at us to return to the house. She stiffly scolded us in front of our friends about crossing the street without supervision. Fortunately our friends also understood the situation and took it in stride. We were not seriously embarrassed and quickly returned while she watched the traffic, likely with some private feelings of concern. We realized that she thought of us as being perhaps four years of age and unaware of traffic. I was in my thirteenth year. We pleaded with her to let us cross back over the street so to continue playing. She obliged. It may have helped her in regaining some orientation. Some of her former understanding was coming back. Recovery slowly eased matters for the family but it never caught up to her earlier excellent health and rigor which had served the nature of active boys.

Mom wrestled within herself to engage with the lives of her three 'boys' - teen agers merging into adults. She was limited somewhat by disabilities from the 'Accident' that would never go away. Nevertheless, there was no 'quit' for her. Often she would bake cookies or cakes to satisfy the family sweet tooth. Sometimes they were the ugliest pastries one might imagine and ineffective to meet the sweet tooth yearnings. They might be mixed with food coloring that induced odd hues not seen in fresh food. Some were lopsided, appearing as if they would topple over if touched. On one occasion she made blue/green colored mayonnaise cookies that possessed much of the major ingredient, never intended for cookies, and should not have had any of it in any event. Brother, Arnie, came in, saw the oddity, and decided to pour himself a glass of milk to cover the strange looking treat. His first bite generated an automatic reflex as he sought a way to expel the offending substance. His facial expressions revealed to the rest of us that the cookies should be avoided in any way possible, but remain respectful to our Mother – as we always meant to do. Somehow, we managed. In the passing of time and with better chosen ingredients in experimentation, she began making tasteful snacks which we appreciated.

Looking back we now see the events as labors of love for her family. We learned something of compassion and the meaning she gave to love in service to us. The improvement in baking revealed that she was truly getting better. We felt thankful. So it was that our family moved along in a new pattern, and better in some overarching way than before the 'Accident.' My parent's testimony made me realize that all matters between persons were open to reconciliation and new ways for us.

All of us knew the family context before and the change that occurred. I soon lost my childhood timidity in taking on some responsibility. I became more outgoing and better able to engage with my classmates even if they were from more affluent families with more 'stuff' and privileges. One of them was Don Libby. His father worked as an engineer monitoring the Oroville Dam while his mother was a secretary for the California State Parks and Recreation.

Both of his parents were highly engaged in the welfare of their children and influential in church functions. Even though we had those 'funny' economic differences, sometimes felt, Don and I shared similar interests in just about everything. We rooted for the same sports teams and went to the same church. The uncertainties of the middle growing up years were fading. Differences dissolved when true friendship was achieved. The adaptations with the similarities were good for life forming. There was an underlying spiritual concept that made for an equality meaning in our lives. Kids don't care 'that much' about affluence and poverty until the prejudices of the adults are carried over to them.

Family, Church, school and friends occupied and formed my life during this period. All rose up in good and nurturing fashion. It may be so for all children in the majority of homes in America, where peace and love have made the normal environment. It appears easy when cast in words on paper, but we seem often to lose our way in self-interests making life burdensome and difficult, and sometimes deviant. We may also be distracted by the publicity given to the misfits in the media. Matters may be better than they seem for most families. Do we really know where we are and the better place in the progression of life? I believe it is better than it is reported. Each person has his/her own story. The 'norm' never quite fits, or seldom does. Each person makes his or her own way.

At Central School our home room teacher in '69 was Miss Rucker. She was a no nonsense teacher who would not put up with any "Tom Foolery." Don sat behind me. I found it extremely difficult to avoid turning around and talking with him. When I did and she observed the violation, Miss Rucker informed me that I needed to stand for a while outside by the door. Don was sent to the other door of the classroom to stand there. With mutual punishment observed, and taken bravely, we were drawn even closer in friendship. We dissolved some of our severe punishment with some smiles and snickers – not much guilt. But, the discipline served for education, and practiced for order in society. Some kids believed we were naughty. Others believed we were brave. It all dissolved in our friendship for Don and Ron.

Don was an inspiration to me and a peer comrade I looked to for confirmation. He provided direction for a lad among his peers seeking confidence and direction while living in a world that appeared to pull in different directions – or so it seemed to the two of us. Perhaps there was something of the rebel in us that was harnessed. At least it worked for us and built a library of memories. The culture seemed taken by a common malady pattern. It was a world influenced by Timothy Leary who encouraged drug use to "find God." The young people idolized the

Beatles album Sargent Pepper's Lonely Hearts Club Band. It was the year of Woodstock that made Rock Music more famous than Jazz. The top movies were The Wild Bunch, Butch Cassidy and the Sundance Kid, Easy Rider, and Midnight Cowboy. There was a strong rebel spirit beckoning my generation. It was a time of confusion for a young teenage boy attempting to find the right direction for life with his family and friends. The church and the world sent contradicting signals. We were responsive to both in some factors. Don knew the better way and encouraged me to follow and not succumb to influences that led to melancholy and loss.

I believe we found the better pattern. Reflection now makes me even more certain of it. Our models were popular too – in ways that were lasting to our lives. A loving family, value oriented friends, caring teachers, and a serving church in a free country were excellent influences to form my young life. I continue to believe in the menu. In later life challenges and errors the background served me well in finding life meaning and fulfillment. The main road always beckoned, and my detours did not serve me well.

Sports did maintain interest for me even if not occupying as much time as formerly. Family had come to mean first interest for me and my brothers. Even so we suffered through the playoff loss of the Oakland Raiders to the Kansas City Chiefs who went on to defeat the Minnesota Vikings in the Super Bowl. We focused on the hard working Miracle Mets who won the World Series. We celebrated the first moon walk by Neil Armstrong and Buzz Aldrin. That seemed like heroic sports – a race into space with the playing field on the moon. (Armstrong hit a golf ball from the moon surface. It may have been the longest drive in history in that there was no air resistance in flight. I wish I knew how far it went.) We breathed sighs of relief as Apollo 13 made it back to earth after equipment malfunctions. My friend Don, by firm choice, focused on the academic meaning of it all and encouraged me to do the same. I seemed to be joined to the best of popular culture, with friends interested in substantive issues. Our pals help make us. My Math interests likely helped. If we 'feel' our gifts we do better.

There were others in my class who were equal examples of academic prowess. One in particular was Kirk Göhre, who even at that age displayed a gift in science. He would often invite me to his home in the foothills east of Oroville. He and his brother had a striking butterfly collection that drew my interest. I was intrigued by how they were able to catch them without damaging their wings. The butterflies were mounted under glass panes with their scientific identification labels posted. They were perfectly and beautifully preserved for display. I was being challenged by my peers to be constructive in interests and conduct. I was choosing the right friends. I too wanted something worthwhile. The concern ought to be primary for serious search of the knowledge of the World and life. My interests early on were toward athletics, and physical skills. The intellectual interests were always there and were emerging stronger. Young students learn more when engaged in interaction with their peer group, but it only works well when the right friends are in the circle of interest. That too became a gift for me in forming my life and meaning. In spite of poverty and a life–changing disaster, I was on my way.

Society ought to do more in exposing the intellectual challenges in friendship groups with exciting learning pursuits. I am benefitted that my friends came from wholesome environments that fostered affirmations for our lives. I would like to believe I made some contributions to them.

We had time for fun. In the back of the family property there was a small irrigation canal where we would often go frog "gigging." The tools were very simple, a pole about 6 feet long with a three pronged metal fork that was four inches wide, and a bag to hold the frogs. After catching a few we took them home for a frog-leg fry. They were publicly touted to be a delicacy. I don't think I prepared them correctly. They tasted like bland chicken at best, and we didn't often have them at their best. Perhaps also, I didn't always prepare them at their best. I had no frog-leg cook book. I felt I was not cut out to be a chef. (Years later I proved that statement – not to others but to myself.) It had to be something 'else' for me. But we did have fun.

On one excursion, we stumbled upon a rattle snake about three feet in length. Friend Kirk quickly sprang into action and "gigged" the reptile near mid body. Raising the pole his captive wriggled violently in the air even striking at the pole several times. With the rattles chanting warnings, Kirk in a bit of panic started towards me yelling to hit it with a rock. My natural response was to run from him and the suffering irate serpent. I finally found a comfortable clearance and sensed that my friend was in peril for a strike target from a sizeable rattlesnake.

Gathering my wits, I returned to assist in his distress and give aid in gaining an imminent demise of the snake. The battle ensued. The snake seemed to become even more enraged, and we more anxious. It became a funny/foolish thing boys do in such escapades. After much yelling and excitement, a stunning blow to the snake's head brought on some composure in 'brave' boys.

Even then the snake continued to twitch. We regained bravery and pummeled it with stone weapons. All was silent following final victory in battle. We pondered the possibility of trying snake meat with frog legs but thought better of it. We had not yet mastered the best preparation of frog legs for meals. What would snake meat do for us? The creature seemed badly bruised so likely would not have served well as the delicacy it was reputed to be. So ended another foray into the exotic small world of kids. Boys will be boys – sometimes incomprehensible, even dangerous, and sometimes foolish. However, the events stay vivid in our memories. It made philosophers of us in menus – from bee honey to snake meat.

Life was becoming more serious for 'growing-up kids.' I found that I enjoyed going to school at Central largely because of caring teachers and agreeable classmates. I even wanted to go early to school so to hang out with my friends, Garrett Jackson and Marvin McKenzie among others. Garrett and Marvin were in the same classroom at Bird Street School but not at Central.

However we were all at Central at different class levels. We would arrive 45 minutes or so before school to play catch with a baseball or football. You have already detected from my story that we shared the love of sports including some participation and knew the importance of practice. It is a legitimate way to use up youthful energy. We interacted in discussion on the latest sporting news usually initiated by Garrett who regularly brought copies of the "Sporting Green" from the San Francisco Chronicle. Somehow he was able to finagle this section from his Dad and bring it with him for the rest of us to read. We devoured it. We were scholars in research of the great game of baseball. This section was a sports and math junkie's paradise. It recited statistics, box scores, standings, and leader boards for the particular sporting season be it football, basketball, golf, hockey or baseball. We were walking computers, especially of baseball lore. It was an extension of my younger years in Grass Valley. There was a wholesome context to it all. It remains for many youths, but is missed by many who seem to get the news coverage for a lot of nonsense, even tragedy. Our management of baseball statistics improved our mastery of mathematics at school – and elsewhere.

Our mornings were filled with debates and discussions over the latest sporting news; such as the Curt Flood and Ritchie Allen trade between the St. Louis Cardinals and the Philadelphia Phillies. Flood would not report to the Phillies reasoning that he was not a "piece of property to be traded and sold irrespective of his wishes." We discussed whether Mr. Flood was correct or not and what his actions would mean to Baseball. As it turned out his case eventually ended in the Supreme Court of the United States where the judges did not rule in his favor. However, through his efforts, Major League Baseball agreed to the "10/5 Rule" which permits players with ten years of Major League Service, the last five with the same team, to veto any trade. We were awakened to the financial and political aspects of a simple sport called baseball. That too is a part of education – especially if one has the Sports Green. It was more than a game it was also a business which changed some of the idealism found in pure love of the sport. We tried to understand it all just as the grown up sportsman seemed to be trying to do. Even sports information was making 'students' of us. It was great for applied Math relating to interests in simple life experience engaging the mind seeking truths about matters a thinking person values. Central School was not only a time to understand social behaviors but also to take seriously the importance of academia. I presume that was more important to parents and teachers than baseball. What we learned in theory fit in many contexts – just the way it is meant to be.

One of the great inspirations and motivations about school at this time was learning about government, society, and the duties of citizens. During those days students could not graduate from the 8th grade unless they passed the "Civics" exam. One could pass all the other classes but if they failed Civics, they would be required to go to Summer School and take the course again if they were to move on educationally. It served to make improved citizens of us. Happily for me, I passed on first try. That achievement was because of a dry, stoic, elderly lady who took her job seriously. She was assigned the task of teaching both American History and Civics. Even though I don't recall her name, and she was not as colorful in personality as other teachers, she nevertheless stressed the importance of learning the subject so that we would become better citizens. Her approach was a methodical presentation that established a base that made it easy to understand where we came from and why we are where we are today as a changing nation.

There was always intimation that we could make America, perhaps the world, even better. We learned that today's actions have consequences for tomorrow. Most importantly, I gleaned that we can shape our future, if we are properly informed and planning our direction. The decline in Civics accents seems to have weakened our citizenship duties including the quality of voting in America. Our concepts of democracy, law and freedom have declined somewhat, or seems to have done so. Our news reporting suggests so. I would raise the banner for a required course in Civics for every American student and persons seeking citizenship. Democracy requires effective personal citizenship if it is to be the guard of freedom. It requires public objective education if the public is to participate in government held responsibility for freedom.

It was during this period that I began seriously to plan my future, understanding that it would take hard work and determination to achieve worthwhile goals and life. My hope and first goal was to be a Major League Baseball player. I was willing to do what it took to achieve baseball's highest objectives. Proceeding in my review I studied about the factors that formed effective athletes. Early in my designs I learned there is also an element of gifting divinely planted to obtain objectives above ordinary standards. It is not enough to be good at what one does. The call is always to excellence, if dreams are to become reality.

The gifting concept belongs to any person in any field. With it we also learn that we enjoy what we do in contribution of service to mankind. That awareness is important if we will be able to ultimately say we enjoyed life. In discovery of what I came to see as my gifts, I determined that Baseball was not in my future not because of unwillingness to work for it but rather there was something else that lay ahead that would utilize my personal gifts, whatever that objective might require. In that context there would initiate passion to appreciation for life objectives, work that would offer something to me and society that would exceed anything I might gain in baseball.

The dream was something emerging that suggested my talents were to be cultivated in another direction. My mind and heart was pointing to a different course that better represented me, the truth about me, and it would make all the difference. However, I will never 'put down' my early ideal to be a big leaguer. It taught me that it is good to have a dream. Out of that initial perception the desire was gaining direction. If this first foray was not to be reality, I needed to find the one that fitted, and make life what it is meant to be for a person – and to some degree, for persons related to that person. It is not always a lonely journey, although some are forced to make it alone. And, there are lonely moments for everyone along the way. What we do always affects others for good or ill. Group success comes from individuals who are willing to excel for the betterment of their group and individual success comes from the group's willingness to contribute. When combined there is teamwork, sometimes unrecognized, that overcomes limitations on the journey to the goal. No matter what the field chosen may be, I learned that it relates to: "Batter up!" If it is the right game on the right field, there will be a hit – sometimes a single, perhaps a double, even a three bagger. Sometimes it's a home run. This last offers some ecstasy. Our dreams shout at us.

*The stretch of road where my parents "Accident" occurred in Taylorsville, California that changed the course of our lives.*

# 6
# *Winning and Losing to Win*

*"Never assume you have it made. Life does not permit a lot of coasting."*
**Coach Brown**

He was a man of athletic proportions, thickly formed in body and appearance, well assembled physically but not overweight. His ruddiness contributed to his title identifying him as "Coach Brown." Along with his warrior-like appearance he exuded an air of confidence that inspired students and players in our school to believe they could rise to high levels of achievement. I am 'proud' to say he was my coach. We all liked him, and worked to achieve his challenges and approval.

Like most aspiring youthful sports enthusiasts and desiring to play out fantasies of greatness, I decided to go out for freshman football my first year at Las Plumas High School. Even though I made the team and went to every practice, that year it proved futile to my dreams of being the next Dick Butkus. I never participated in a single play of any of the games. My role appeared to be practice – a lot. Weighing 95 pounds and growing weary of being pushed around by beefy players, I concluded that football was not my game. I abandoned football dreams and was content to wait for baseball season where skill, not size of the athletes dominated. I maintained a belief there was someplace for me. There was a lingering 'fire' in the belly attitude.

Our new sport for the next three weeks in the physical education class was boxing. Coach Brown had us line up by size and weight so that he could pair us off according to the stipulated weight ranges permitted for competition – so to make a level field for competition. Since my friend Marty Kent and I were the smallest in the class, we thought we would be paired first.

Instead he started with bigger kids and worked his way down the scale to us. Marty and I were last, but Coach Brown seemed to give quality time with us. He was a 'level field' coach for every student. My group was gratified, even if we were the little guys on the team. With clipboard in hand, he asked if we thought about trying out for the wrestling team. He continued by telling us that he had an opening at the 95 pound class and that if we went out for the team one of us would immediately go to the varsity, the other to Junior - varsity. Either way it meant we would receive a "Letter" in a sport and could wear a "Lettermen's Jacket." To a young athlete, this jacket was a symbol of graduation into manhood. I am told this feeling of belonging is common across the country – then and now. More importantly it meant we would participate in tournaments in fair competition – win or lose.

We were intimidated by this massive figure, but admired, 'Coach Brown,' who pressed his points both Marty and I stammered that we would need to discuss it with our parents. Marty told me later that he did not want to. But, the idea intrigued me. My projection was that it would give me something to do during winter season in athletics, while I waited for baseball to begin in the spring. Further the 'Letter' and the 'Jacket' loomed up in my mind and pride. It seemed like a win-win situation for me. I stayed a few minutes after school to watch the team practice for a short time and then went home to discuss the idea with my Dad. Unaware that scholastic wrestling was quite different than the wrestling seen on TV, he expressed concern that he did not want to see my head "smashed" on the turn buckle of the ring, or be hit in the back with an auditorium chair. He held out by saying, "Ronnie, you're too small for those big boys." I was caught between my Dad and Coach Brown – one encouraging and one discouraging.

The next day at P.E., I expressed my father's concern to Coach Brown who in turn just smiled and advised me to invite him to the next match the following Wednesday. Good thinking. After nagging and coaxing, I persuaded Dad to relent and we went to the event to see what it was all about. As we watched the junior varsity match, Dad realized that his fears were unwarranted. It was nothing like the entertaining performances he had viewed on television. No turn buckles and no auditorium chairs were being used as weapons. Here was a genuine sport. The referee was in control and there were no incidents or distractions to permit "behind-the-back" shenanigans. Orderly processes were invoked with thirteen different weight classes, each waiting their turn and pulling for each other in respectful competition. Individual match scores were kept with the winner gaining points for their team. Wrestling matches at this level is for the one and the many – for the individual and the team. It was exhilarating as we watched the excitement and intensity of the match. There was idealism in it, far from the crudity of the TV episodes of alleged wrestling. In this the youths of school have it better than adults. Have adults lost something in this and other venues that invite violence if the rules are lost?

It came time for the Varsity to engage. Before they did, introductions were in order. Each team stood in line opposite each other on the edge of the mat. After each competitor was announced they would run to the center of the mat and await the announcement of their opponent then they would shake hands and await their signal to 'battle.' Clean competition became part of my education.

The first weight class, and the lightest, to be announced was 95 pounds. The boy from Willows High School went to the center of the mat but no one from Las Plumas appeared to oppose him. By default, he received the maximum amount of six points for his team. As his hand was raised in the air to receive a forfeit, I informed my Dad that he would have been my opponent. He then turned to me: "Ronnie, I think you could 'whup' him." At that moment I realized that he was all for my new athletic career, but more importantly he demonstrated confidence in me that helped me to believe I could do it. This is partly what dads are for. As it turned out the boy's name in the default match was Dan Hall who later qualified to go to the State Tournament. He had a fancy leg ride and a 'killer' guillotine maneuver that caused a lot of anguish to his opponents. All of this was genuine, skillful and in fun. It was great!

So it was that I became a wrestler, albeit at 95 pounds. I would never make it to Sumo – so popular in Japan. Practices were highly structured with allotments of time for stretching, learning new moves, practicing them, and finally to develop physical and mental conditioning. Coach kept the practices moving and I looked forward to each one. He instilled the importance of team effort. On the surface level wrestling appears to be an individual sport but the underlying element is understanding that singular success ultimately comes from the group as a whole. It is a magnificent dichotomy. Alone on the mat the wrestler can claim lone success if victorious but can blame no one else if opportunities are missed or mistakes are made. However, his teammates and coaches are there for encouragement and direction. We really learned loyalty and togetherness. We went home with a team score. Wrestling is a demanding sport that requires strict discipline in not only stamina but in health maintenance. Because of weight concerns, the individual has constantly to be cognizant of calorie intake. If over the weight limit, the grappler will have to move up to the next weight class. That often means a vacancy appears resulting in a forfeit with easy points going to the other team.

Wrestling students in the lower weight classes were seldom seen in the cafeteria during lunch. Instead they might be running in the gym to lose weight. As hours approached for 'weigh in', wrestlers were seen jogging in place and spitting into towels – anything to meet the judgment of the scale. During my day, rubber suits were worn (It is now a violation) to gain an advantage through sweating to achieve weight loss during training periods. I discovered that true wrestlers are the most dedicated and disciplined athletes of any sport I know about. Those that engage understand that it is individual hard work and preparation that brings success for the team as well as the wrestler. I am pleased my experience took me to the wrestlers' mat.

My first match was with Lassen High School from Susanville, CA. Since Lassen was the visiting team they were given the first opportunity to warm up. Each wrestler wore a bright yellow uniform that consisted of sweat pants and shirt. The team came jogging out of the locker room clapping their hands in cadence and then proceeded to circle the mat several times before settling in to well-timed clapping of the hands - ending with their hands to their thighs and a firm stance. Each one looked determined and focused on the 'battle' that was about to occur. After some spirited stretching they huddled in the center and there was silence. A few moments later with a shout they burst out by arching backward with only the top of their heads and the bottom of their feet touching the mat. Then with a quick spin on their heads, they rotated to where only heads and toes were touching the surface. It had the appearance of a flower in bloom from a time enhanced camera. It was quite impressive. Their procedure suggested winners, well coached. No athletes were better formed in bodies than wrestlers in either high school or college. They were also less likely to be ignored. Wrestling is perforce, a body builder.

Our warm up was less showy, with less fanfare. We quietly stretched and practiced a few moves. I preferred our method so to save my energy for the match. As we lined across from each other my opponent, Dwayne Chandler, was announced. Immediately he bolted to the center of the mat waiting for me. As my name was announced, I could not help but feel a sense of recognition in front of Dad who was watching in the stands. I was confident that I was going to do well as I jogged to the center to meet Dwayne. With a firm grip, he quickly placed both his hands around my extended hand and with the same speed backed quickly to the mark on the smaller circle in the center of the mat. I went back to mine and waited for the referee to blow the whistle to begin the match. In all it was quite a show, even though no wrestling had yet been done.

With speed and precision, Chandler lunged successfully for my legs and I being in full retreat, he circled behind me to gain control. Underneath him I quickly responded from what I learned in practice to stand up – if possible. Instead of standing, gaining a position on my part, he pushed me back down and we tumbled out of bounds. The referee blew his whistle to stop the action and we returned to the center of the mat where two parallel lines lay about eighteen inches apart.

Because he had gained control, I was instructed to place my hands in front of one line and my knees behind the other. Once I was in position, the referee directed Chandler to place one of his hands on my elbow and the other around my waist on my belly.

After getting in position, I thought I would try the "whizzer" move to gain an advantage. The move is to stand up and at the same time my arm was to circle back to hook my opponent under the arm pit. If completed successfully, it would free me from an inferior position to one of equality and eventually to gaining control of him – that's if all went well and as practiced. If successful I would earn a point.

The whistle sounded, I began to raise my right leg and circled my left arm to his right armpit with success. However, he countered by circling his left arm around my neck in a 'half nelson' and with his right arm already looped around my waist, he flipped me to a position where I was laying prone on my back. Disabled from any movement on my part, he solidified his grip around me; so much so that I felt as if I were a fly, trapped in the web of a spider awaiting my ultimate demise. As he seemingly attempted to drive his chest through me to the mat, I realized I was at his mercy and the only hope for me was that the referee would intercede. After the official slapped the mat indicating a fall, Chandler rose quickly to his feet, went to his former start position and waited for me to reassert and stand up. I did, somewhat dazed. We shook hands, and his arm was raised in triumph by the ref.

Lassen gained six points, the same score as if our team had forfeited. I remembered thinking that I did not contribute at all to the team on that occasion. However, Coach Brown and the entire team were there to greet me when I came off the mat. I had tried against a 'veteran.' They were not disappointed but rather encouraged me with words, "Good job," and "You did great for your first match." Coach comforted me by telling me that my opponent had pinned every one of his opponents during the current year and to not worry about it. "We'll work on it and get him next time." These words instilled confidence and a desire to do whatever was necessary to contribute to my team. About a month later in Susanville, I wrestled Chandler again. He beat me, but instead of a fall it was only a decision where I lost 4-0 and thus only gaining three points for his team instead of six. I was either improving or my veteran opponent was declining. I was determined to do my best.

Through the rest of my days as a wrestler in high school, my back was never again turned towards the mat for a fall or back points. The whole experience served me well. We sometimes lose so to win in the follow–up experiences. I would do it again even with the same outcome. My experience became a parable of life to me. I had lost, but I won. We can achieve that paradox many times.

That year our team finished fourth out of six in the league. Although I personally did not have a winning record, I was able to qualify for the Northern Section finals by finishing fourth in the Subsection Tournament. Placing in that tournament and receiving a ribbon inspired me to continue. I was improving. The 95 pounders had to watch out for Nelms. Winning also helped me learn something about my father and how to gain his attention. Wrestling even affected meaning for me - there was a win–win attitude developed in my family. We all felt a new psychology. The experience is worth review as it formed my life as certainly as did my winning episodes that gained so much team and school attention. Losing can teach us, if we are alert to accept ourselves, and gain an awareness of what is important for life. (But winning seems better – if arrogance is resisted.)

While I was participating in football, Dad stopped attending the games because as he put it "You are wasting my time if you don't get to play." I suppose it was his way of pushing me to higher levels by rewarding me with his attendance or maybe he was embarrassed that other father's kids were playing but his son wasn't. (We both knew I wasn't a 'beefy' guy.) When I started wrestling he would attend the home matches and afterward offer his well -meaning suggestions of how to improve. However, during the early matches when I wasn't winning his attendance declined. When I placed at the Sub-Section tournament, he was present at the Finals. Even though I lost in the first round, I learned that winning would draw him out so I set out to win perhaps to make him proud. This tension related to families is too little understood in the development of children. It is high school level for athletes – sometimes for good and sometimes for bad. Every family should find a way for special recognition for every member of the family to every other family member. Every person 'belongs' somewhere, and we need to enforce that belief. We belong to each other in some ways, and are bereft when these ways are ignored. Too many elders evaluate everything in the terms of winning so lose some opportunity to fortify their children for life competition in which these will be for every person some wins and some losses. Rightly managed, the losses can become wins. Remember the 'Accident.' Our family members all 'showed up' after a fearful loss. Even so my mother paid a highs price for the lesson… She never faulted anyone for the experience.

My father quit school after the 8th grade to work so to assist the family during depression years. The same year I entered High School Dad completed his GED and received his diploma from Oroville High School. This assisted me in my studies both in observing his efforts, and because most of the books I had to use were the same books he had to purchase. The primary benefit to me was that he bought teacher editions that included answers to key questions in the back indexes. This helped me, particularly in Algebra, to know what the answer should be and then work through the problem to gain the understanding of how the answer was found. I had to find the answer I already knew. It served me well. It is a good way to learn – another tool for purpose. That technique is also little used for education, but commonly practiced in business. It even relates to spiritual issues beginning with: How did I get here? Where am I going?

One day the Math teacher, Mr. Savage, overheard me telling one of the other students that I knew the answer to a difficult problem but was having difficulty determining how to get there.

He questioned me how I knew. After disclosing my source, he approved of my method but cautioned against cheating. He was pleased that I was searching for a legitimate procedure to the answer. Education not only means to have the correct answers, but to teach procedures so to arrive at the correct answers.

My grades were good throughout High School and received the accolades from Mom and Dad. I surely could have applied myself more and accomplished more. I suppose every person will say that. Early maturity will help some. It serves proper motivation. Math came to the forefront for me in thought and intent as I began to enjoy solving problems. Even so in the young person the mind and body are always competing for time, expression and loyalty. Sports were my passion, particularly wrestling. But, balance was beckoning. It was becoming serious business – this 'giving up.'

That Spring I went out for JV (Junior Varsity) baseball and made the team even though I didn't play much because there were older players well coached and experienced. I rested my hopes in the future. In my sophomore year I hoped to show my 'stuff.' It would be my year. It wasn't to be. Early in season I made two costly errors in one inning and was promptly returned to the bench. I was not called on again. While watching the other players, I came to the conclusion that even though I loved baseball, my talent didn't seem to lay there. At least I had gained a love of active games, a love that remains with me into my adult years. The love of the game seems greater in persons who participated at some level, successful in performance – or not. The interest is a healthy distraction from the rigors of the requirements of life order, and becomes a part of that order.

During the same season I was playing Baseball; on Saturdays Coach Brown recruited some parents, including Dad, and we would drive a team of wrestlers to either Sacramento or the Bay Area to participate in AAU (Amateur Athletic Union) tournaments. I did quite well at those tournaments winning some and placing in others. Searching for recognition from Dad coupled with doing well in wrestling and not so well in baseball, the logical choice was to pass on baseball and focus my efforts toward wrestling. Why not choose the winning context? Makes sense: good sense. I was in a game to win, not only in the role of playing by respected rules, but winning with my family. There was more to the matter than just wrestling – as there usually is for kids seeking some recognition - approval, a sign of success. At 95 pounds, wrestling was it!

After school instead of going to baseball practice, I would lift weights and run several miles. I would also grab anybody I could find to practice my moves. During moments of solitude the interest guided me to dream and plan for what I wanted to do. My immediate objective was to become League Champion in wrestling and go to the State Tournament. The search for my personal gifts was through learning to play by the rules and the circumstances to achievement. The books gave the rules, the opponents the circumstances. The opposing wrestler was seeking the same outcome that I was working for. That made us respect each other. All that is a 'school' in itself – a teacher of life formation.

In order to help pay for those tournament trips and have some extra spending money, I took a job on Friday evenings and Sunday afternoons washing dishes at Thrifty's Coffee Shop. It proved tempting to be around all the food and drinks while I was trying to maintain my weight for the tournaments. It was a test in self-control. However, during the summer I worked full time and didn't concern myself as much with the weight issue. When the manager went home for the day, we would make sandwiches that Dagwood would envy. Dagwood and Blondie were popular – from a comic strip in the newspaper 'funnies'. Elaborate sandwiches became known as 'Dagwoods.' We became quite creative with tomato, onion, pickles topped on bacon, ham, roast beef, and hamburger with a melting slice of different cheeses between each layer; not to mention a bun that cut in half looked like lively bookends. All that made one sandwich. (God, parents, doctors and nutrition people forbid.)

All the Football and Cross Country athletes were encouraged to take P.E. during 7th period which was the last class of the day. During this time they would give a course on weight lifting and endurance. Coach Brown was able to arrange for me a 6th period free time (it was supposed to be for study hall) and 7th period P.E. His 6th period was free as well so we would jog what was known at the time as the "Hill Course." It mapped 5 miles of steep hills which started and ended at the school. After coming back from this heart pounding journey he would encourage me to run another 3 miles on the school's cross country course while he would go in and prepare for the next class.

About the time I would finish the run; P.E would start with weight lifting and end with a mile run around the track where we would be cajoled to finish in less than six minutes. I am proud to say that I was able to accomplish this despite the previous 8 mile run and the weight lifting. After P.E., I would spend the next hour or so practicing moves with Fred Jenkins. It was clear to me that I had found the answer in eating and running for the good life. It certainly contributed to a healthy body.

Fred Jenkins was my good friend in those early days at Central and continues today to engage my life. He blames me for getting him into this demanding sport to which blame I take full credit. Fred not only wrestled at Las Plumas but went on to U.C. Davis and became an All American. But most importantly he had extreme compassion for an exuberate dreamer. Eat a little, and run a lot. It served both of us well.

During my junior year, Coach Brown was setting the foundation for a successful wrestling program that would last several years, one that would not only win league championships but also North Section Titles. It would be the first time since its inception in 1962 that Las Plumas High School would know such success and may not have known since. He began by recruiting Coaches Boone and Brett. Boone was a guidance counselor and Brett was a student teacher who later became head coach at Chico State University. They knew their 'stuff.' I was coached by devoted coaches of excellence. They made up for some omissions in student families.

Along with his coaches, Brown recruited the student athletes that had tenacious attitudes and a thirst for winning. Along with Jenkins he recruited Dewey Travis who later came in second at the California State Tournament; Scott Fairly, who was a three sport athlete; Mike Paul, who had a lot of spunk and an attitude of confidence about him that would tend to irritate one to greatness just to spite him; Don Adams, who was an intellectual workaholic that analyzed everything; Shane Walters, who we dubbed "Baby Bull" and later took over the program at Las Plumas; and, Chuck Butterfield who was our gentle giant that is now a football referee in the Big Sky Conference. There were of course others that contributed greatly to what was a vision for the program. All of them have gone on and have led productive lives partly due to the lessons learned in the wrestling program generated by Coach Brown and his staff. I learned that the best part of my athletic experience relates to the discipline of fair and friendly competition in leadership and production of purpose. It was a double benefit: the discipline of the sport, and the inspiration of competent teacher/coaches.

My junior year while wrestling at 112 pounds, we came in second to Lassen in the league with Dewey and me obtaining all-league honors. In order to gain that position, I had to beat a formidable foe from Paradise High, Joe Crabtree. Previously, during my freshman and sophomore years Crabtree dominated me. However, at the beginning of my third year Coach Brown constructed my training program to win the bout with Crabtree. Every time I felt like taking a rest or slough off, I was reminded that was the time to push ahead because my opponent wasn't sloughing off. Besides, if he was, that created an opportunity to get ahead. My focus, my mantra was to beat Crabtree. The first time we met that year he beat me, but I will never forget the first time I won a match with Crabtree. It was at our school auditorium in front of other students and families. My strategy was to get the take down in the first period which would put me up 2-0 and then ride him out. During the second period he reversed my strategy to gain a tie of 2-2. The third period I gained a reversal to win 4-2. The same strategy occurred at the league tournament. However, he turned the table on me at the Section finals. That second place finish gained me a trip to the 1973 State Tournament. Even though I lost to a wrestler from Overfelt High of San Jose, I was energized to work even harder to place at State in my senior year. I felt I was on my way after a great year. Even with some losses, I was winning. It's great to be a 'winner.' With true sportsmanship there is even winning in losing – the experience of life especially in its formation.

Each spring after the State Tournament, Coach Brown organized a healthy contingency of high school wrestlers to compete in AAU tournaments. The core group this year consisted of Fred, Dewey, Mike, Brian Holmes, my brother Arnie and me. These trips energized us in realizing that we could win not only the league but the North Sections. With each match against accomplished wrestlers we became confident that we could compete against the powerhouse schools such as Lassen, Shasta and Anderson.

Not only did we compete but we beat them, winning every tournament and going undefeated with a perfect record. We had five all leaguers; Jenkins, Travis, Walters, Adams and me. However, we only had one Section Champion, Jenkins. The other twelve weight classes our team finished fourth or higher. Quite an accomplishment when measured against more than thirty schools competing. We had joined the 'power house' schools that year.

As for me, I won approximately 30 matches that year while losing three, two of which I believe the referee made bad calls. All persons get bad calls along life's way. 'Water under the bridge' or some would say sour grapes. However, I learned a valuable lesson from Coach Brown. Both times I came off the mat upset at the official for not calling the stall or 'running off the mat' on the competing wrestler. After the third loss, while running the hill section with Coach Brown, he told me that I needed to be so far ahead of my opponent that a bad call from a referee would not make a difference. What a lesson! Prepare to cover the 'bad call' – and win anyway. I could cover myself with an 'extra' effort to cover 'accidents' like an unfair ruling – if one were to take place. Those words have stayed with me through all these years and I have used them to avoid resting on former laurels, but rather strive to improve performance. Something might interfere in the best of plans. He was blunt in telling me the truth that I would dog it the first two rounds and then come alive in the third. He continued that I needed to 'engage' in all three. Never assume you have it 'made.' Life doesn't permit a lot of coasting. I want to give it my best. The other fellow can run his or her own race. I became my own competition. Am I genuine all the way? I learned 'life' that helped me recover after some big life failures years later.

This was evidenced on several occasions when I would be losing going into the third period but then go into a full sprint. I have to admit that I would save my energy for that third period. Maybe it was the heroics of it all or maybe it was because I enjoyed the comeback. My attempt was to have my opponent under estimate my abilities and spring with the element of surprise.

On occasion there is something of a put–down in 'showing up' the opposition. That really doesn't belong. Each person should play his or her own game following the rules – the best to excellence. Persons have their own excellence within themselves. The point is not to let yourself down. If you do, you let your coach down, and your mates, perhaps your family.

On one occasion during an AAU tournament Mike Paul happened to fall in my weight class. Before we were going to wrestle, Mike went to coach and expressed to him that he didn't want to humiliate me. Coach's response was to warn Mike "Don't under estimate Ron, he is a gamer. You are in the match of your life." Mike was basing his assumption upon my method during practice session where I was not so interested in winning each round but rather more interested in perfecting a move. Mike did beat me 1-0 but during the middle of the match when I was attacking, he stopped and pleaded with me and the referee to allow him to use the facilities because evidently he was about to defecate. Seeing that his situation was not going to be a good thing for any of us, we decided to permit a recess. In the years since I have reminded him about the incident and the time 'I kicked the crap out of him.' We always have a good laugh about it.

Disappointment followed me at the end the season. I was rated number one in my class at 130 pounds but because I wanted to do better at the State Tournament, I decided to drop weight to the 123 pounds class. The Friday before Saturday's Sub-Section tournament I became ill. It may have been my own folly that led to the illness. To this day I believe it was because my immune system was down due to the loss of weight. I had to forfeit. It meant that part of my life, on the brink of highest success – was ended. I should have maintained the level I had achieved, win or lose. Sometimes thinking ourselves to be clever, we end up losing – for sure. Often I think how things might have been different had I stayed at 130 pounds. We sometimes out-maneuver our lives. It occurs when undue pride sneaks in on us. In later family experience I 'goofed' again.

After High School we all moved on in our separate scenarios finding where we belonged in the larger world of competition. It wasn't until over thirty five years later that a number of us got together in Oroville to remember the 'glory days' we shared as teammates and competitors.

I remember the feeling that we shared a common goal and achieved it. At the time of our reunion my business had just gone through financial difficulties from the burst of the housing bubble of 2008. I was wandering about in my mind, feeling for direction for some way to turn impending tragedy into recovery. I had experienced the recovery route before. The confidence we remembered in our mutual experiences, in coaching and action fomented a reminder of the confidence and determination that we had about competing and winning. It was a recollection that the pain of hard work brings the joy of success. The challenge was completed with an attitude to face the obstacles with steadfastness and seek ways to overcome and win. Winning attitudes are contagious and that has made all the difference. The lessons I had learned long ago came flooding in. Why had I diluted them during the years?

Of course there were other factors, but the episodes of wrestling experience are fodder for my story here. There were always family, prayer, coaches, and others that cleared the way. It was up to me to learn and apply the teaching factors. The dreams turned into practical application. It is great comfort to have no regrets, and to have friends who served each other in learning about life and dreams to goals. At the root of this attitude is the steadfastness of my wrestling coaches in their interest and participation with students. The elders, something of father figures, became our mentors for life. They were coaches and teachers who not only dictated or cajoled us in what to do but they went beyond the usual effort to inspire students to reach for a kind of greatness in whatever they do. This was meant, not for arrogance but fulfillment. Their enthusiasm was infectious to all those with whom they came in contact, be it lay students or wrestlers. They were deeply involved in our individual lives both socially and personally. To this day they have kept contact with a number of their protégés of which I am one. They deserve a chapter in the story of my life and that too has made all the difference for me. There were times in my life when I mentally, perhaps even spiritually called on Coach Brown. In my functioning he was always present. When that happens, the beneficiaries feel their lives have been decent and worthwhile – meaningful. I sometimes wonder why, when we have been taught and mentored so well, we permit forgetfulness to occupy the best formative years of our lives. So we delay maturity and lose some creativity.

*Getting together with some of my wrestling buddies in 2009 and*
*reminiscing "glory days" where I was reminded of our mutual experiences,*
*confidence and determination that we had about competing and winning.*
*Top Left to right Rhonda Jenkins Murray, Coach Art Brown, Dewey Travis,*
*Andy Graham, Jim Cheatham, Terry Jacobsen, Mike Jacobsen, Coach*
*Ernie Boone, Bottom Left to Right, Fred Jenkins, Scott Fairley, Mike Paul,*
*Mike Hurst, Mike Hedrick, Ron Nelms, and Shane Walters.*

# 7
# *Transitioning*

*"Looking for a narr one,"*
*Vern*

High School life ended for me with complimentary evaluations. I had completed diploma studies rather well, and ranked high on the SAT scores – a test professionally regarded at the time for college entrance. It is purported to be an indication of readiness for college and likelihood of collegiate success. However, personal choices, even for competent students, may not permit follow-through to earning a college degree. Although strongly encouraged to finish college after fitful starts, my personal unguided choices interrupted any straight line to objectives for me. The omissions related to my profiles neutralized the meaning of the testing program.

Even though I stumbled along, I was determined to find an objective for my professional life. That would be the way to happy results for me. I did take the responsibility in my own way, and blame no one for the omissions along the way.

From the SAT test, there emerged suggestions, both implied and obvious, regarding the areas in which the seeking student might be expected to do his or her best and most fulfilling work in an academic major – all leading to professional life and interest. Math was easy for me, and my reviews verified competence in that area. Mathematics is a discipline, sometimes holding highest regard by educators both then and currently, in predicting future academic and professional success. It seemed that everyone in my social circle, including me, believed that I would go on to college. The only barrier appeared to be the cost for higher education, modest in the extreme to present costs, but costly by our standards and circumstances at the time. There were strong hints of future escalating costs – which indeed took place and continue at the time of this writing.

My home life had settled in with my parents, brothers and me. We were drawn together by The Accident that had nearly cost us the lives of Mom and Dad but affecting Mom most seriously - taking years for some normalcy to return, but never total recovery. Matters did change, for Dad and the family with him, and we became united in our Church relationship when he became serious about his own beliefs and life direction – noted especially in the family context and in his personal/professional involvement. That context improved so to turn tragedy into what we believe brought blessing for effective family life. We became a planning and devoted family.

Tragedy can often be turned to blessing to improvement over a former negative position or condition. It did for us. It is partly a consequence for embracing a positive attitude, and faith for life meaning. We were able to take life on. At the time of my high school graduation Mom was functional and determined in her duties, moving along positively in the care of our family. Dad's work would find a better wage and some changes along the way so promising a better economic situation for us. There was a looking-up attitude in us. Domestic life was moving along in the right direction. We were truly a unified family. What a gift that is for children in formation of life. We gained a positive context for our home.

Church life became more important for us, fulfilling in both the life patterns and faith issues of our lives. Our closest friends were there, and for me they included some of my school friends. Other friends, not in the church, were included, but all were wholesome to each other to develop bonds in relationships – especially for me among the athletes related to the wrestling team. That interest served me well, and made an athlete of a scrawny kid guided into a constructive life context by interested teachers and coaches who sought to utilize the talents of students with whom they identified and worked. Their efforts were for the students' benefit, likely also to fulfill them as successful at what they were professionally and personally expected to be and do.

Further we, three brothers growing up, tended to identify with each other affirmatively. Life seemed good to us. Again – we became a bonded family, loving and respecting each other. That is what families are meant to accomplish. Society is rightly concerned when the family is fractured. Family solidarity is vital to workable societies and the cultivation of affirmative values. We tend to take on family solidarity without understanding the process, so we may not take it on when we grow up. Something escapes us. It is a common problem for satisfying destiny.

Puberty development hung heavily for us, but mostly in private personal context even when it had its public impact on our speech registers and the ongoing issues of bodily development. As life moves along we joke about it. The saying goes: The lad's been shaving for two years, and cut himself both times. Most persons muddle through the physical and psychological maturing years without much help or meaningful understanding about what is happening to them. Persons seem to fuss their way through the period. Most families don't seem prepared to accomplish the transition as satisfactorily as it ought to be addressed. The general California culture does not prove helpful in developing serious life approaches in early years. The weather is too salubrious to rein in the casual lifestyle. We do not apply easily the concept of planning our lives, and living out a plan. As a result there is a leap here, a leap to there, perhaps back again – and so the story goes. We ought to do better. Society does not manage the puberty period well for young people. For their guidance and the building of a better youthful transition we ought to do better than we do from about twelve to twenty one years. This is basically a family matter, but affects society generally at great cost. Some believe that this casualness in the family is the cause for much of society's problem culture. We tend to cause trouble for ourselves and society during this young adult life transition.

We graduate from high school. The day before we were children managed in part by our parents, but somewhat naïve about life and the world – even while we were engaged in our lives with others and informed about some factors, for family and community. We were dependent.

The day after graduation we are grown-up and it is expected that we will take responsibility for ourselves. Lunch isn't free anymore. Parents must turn their energies to making sure they have some retirement security. That common transitional maneuver is a long trip to traverse in 48 hours for grown-up children. It is made in lightning speed. Youths seem to be animated but many seem to be on another planet. Some handle transition well, some so-so, and some lose direction on the road to morality, responsibility and integrity. It is some distance from high school to maturity. There may be drifting and that can last for short or long periods of time – perhaps for years while matters are being sifted out. Some youths are never really harnessed to responsibility. This transition time is filtered through various attitudes, experiences, hits and misses, changes and habits, grasping-for and letting-go. We either grow up – or we don't. It is up to us even though we are young and not really prepared for the ride of life. All of this is serious to our meaning as persons. Our futures are forming long before we leave the home of our childhood. Youth often misses because of impatience and impractical decisions necessary for later life.

Sophisticated moderns tend to manage it by sending their children off to college for the big transition to adult life. Usually they would like for their children to go off to higher education and training even if the kid is not warming to the idea and high school experience has not indicated that it would be feasible to try for a degree. College is presently talked about in advance in nearly all but the poorest families, and taken as a general expectation so that the experience of college is believed to be a must if persons are to be considered for professional appointments - even for jobs that do not draw upon the collegiate experience. College does tend to improve relationships even for the most modest professions. Studies suggest that most collegians do find better points of view for work and public life, and marriage solidarity, than those who do not extend education beyond high school. Currently students and parents take on monumental debt to gain a collegiate degree. Some of these students, we are informed, will never pay the debt that they have incurred, and will, in the meantime, limit their adult options because of monetary obligations forced to first consideration. Each person must find the answer for self and the future. That future can become elusive. It requires determination, sacrifice, and some vision. In twenty–something young adults entering professional life with a huge debt makes different persons of them

- especially in attitude. There must be a better economical way to launch personal life and family for those young adults. The secret may be that young adults be mentored by caring adults to follow a pattern of planning to achieve some ambition to meaning for life. More and more colleges are finding ways to help their students with the costs of education.

In our youth, taken with the contradictions and paradoxes of our lives, and naiveté about the context of our place in the world, we launch even feebly, with some ambition and altruism – to seek occupation so to become meaningful in society and gratified with self. With all that has gone on in our lives before this juncture, we have seldom been adequately prepared to make the transitions necessary for high school youths to become serious adults with modern responsibilities. The point is that prepared or not, we have to make the transitions to responsibility and wisdom. It takes some living and self-imposed limitations to achieve success. It becomes increasingly difficult because of the spread of change. As once change came slowly, it is now too fast for the masses.

My approach to independent life was to assume that I would go to college and emerge with an academic degree. Because my early aspiration for a baseball career was dashed, I considered it my duty to life and society to become a high school teacher and wrestling coach. My SAT scores were high, but my grade point average was somewhat lower placing me on the alternate list for California State Scholarships – good but not great. I was awarded $250 from the David Purvis Memorial scholarship. Even though I appreciated the gift from that family, it was not sufficient to meet the $3,000 required yearly for attending Point Loma Nazarene College in San Diego. There were other expenses related to room and board to be factored in. What is a poor boy supposed to do? Some of the hope is diluted in the concern not only for tuition but the additional significant costs for life maintenance.

Point Loma was counted the ideal place for all college bound parishioners from our church. Most of the kids in our youth group, including my buddy Don Libby, were planning to attend in the fall, 1974. Since I did not receive an adequate scholarship, I was somewhat content with working as a short order cook at Thrifty's Coffee Shop to pay for an anticipated education at

Chico State University – just up the road from home. Attending Chico I could remain at home and reduce maintenance expenses. I even thought about wrestling for the University as a walk on candidate for the team with the hope of obtaining an athletic scholarship. However in the spring of 1974, a business man and his wife from our church, Larry and JoAnn Tomlinson, offered to pay for my education if I chose to go to Point Loma. Jumping at the opportunity, I sent my letter of intent to the school. It was heady for me to anticipate adult life and on my own – off to college.

Larry and JoAnn thought it was important that I receive not only a scholastic education but also be formally cultivated in Christian values. Larry was an accomplished entrepreneur who at the time sold mobile homes in Oroville. They were good friends of our family and took deep interest in our welfare. Mom would often babysit their two toddlers, Barry and Todd. I discovered from her efforts and influence that I liked kids. Sometimes I would assist her. I enjoyed playing with them to feel their joys. Being ever creative in odd ways, I would sometimes coax the lads to put underwear on their heads. With hair sticking through the leg holes, they resembled characters from a Dr. Seuss novel. I thought it was quite amusing and fun for the boys. Mom did not always share my sense of humor. I was only trying to help in my own way, even if frivolous. (I still believe my antics served well – at least for little kids.) They liked it.

A letter arrived from the State of California awarding me a scholarship to pay for tuition. At the same time I learned that Point Loma was dropping its wrestling program. Disappointed, I decided to enroll anyway hoping the program might be reinstated. It wasn't. I was off to Point Loma College with mixed feelings. Motivation was diluted somewhat. Not all my college vision was going to be met. It may have made a difference in my higher education experience and life direction. Sports had helped me to maintain interest in finishing High School. The pattern is quite common for students in extra – curricular programs. It related to youth, required clean living, took up young energy for good purpose and was popular.

Arriving at the College in the fall, 1974, one year after its move from Pasadena's inland valley to ocean beaches, I was awed by the panoramic view and the ever changing sunsets over the Pacific Ocean. My life had always been in the great inland valley of California. The new environment gave one a sense of being in a section of paradise. Some might believe the surroundings distracting for study. That was not the case for us, and students adapted well to the beauty of nature that included great waters. The weather was almost always ideal. I found that it stimulated the thought process and caused me to dig deeper into understanding about life and learning. Nature made me more serious about my human existence and meaning. Chapel was designed for Christian life formation. I was moving along even if I did not have all the pieces in place. Wherever I went I felt the call of nature – the out-of-doors as life context. There was vision in it, but blurred. It was not distracting, but beckoning. It would become an important factor for me.

During those days, before computers dominated, we would have to be physically present in the auditorium to enroll for courses. Since classes were limited in size, it often became a first come first serve order. The Dean would open the doors and seniors would go first so preceding the other students in registration. The juniors would then follow with sophomores and freshman completing the competition for class choices. The students would hustle to a table that represented a specific department and courses with preferred professors. At that table they would request to sign up for the classes they wanted. Not knowing what to list as my major,

I arrived a day early and took advantage of the opportunity to speak to an advisor. To my surprise, he informed me that I scored in the top five percent in the nation for Math and encouraged me to focus on Math/Engineering. Further, he advised me to begin by taking first year calculus. I was really at an advantage, what with affinity for an area many students evaded, but highly respected by academicians. I seemed to have a step up – if I wanted to take it.

While in High School, I had the privilege of attending Math and Science classes with some bright students – like my buddies Jenkins, Göhre and Adams; but I never thought of myself on their level. So it surprised me to hear that I was in league with my old, better funded friends, even though at a distant college. It lifted my self- esteem. Persuaded by the counselor that my strength was Math, I compromised and took a Pre-Calculus class in the fall along with Physics and Chemistry. But in my ruminations I felt there was something missing. At the time I wasn't sure what it was but it was an unexplainable restlessness for something outside academia. Sports interest may have had something to do with that. Many students have the feeling. They may quit, or press on without adequate fulfillment. I am told this is common for young people emerging from an active childhood like mine that relates to nature and strenuous physical activity in sports. The body has to adjust to sedentary postures for reading and writing. Even so I learned to love reading and have also been told I engage in it more than most men. It is an appreciated gift for me. It contributes strongly to life.

Youth, with its exuberance carries with it forms of impatience. It is fomented by eager desire to apply the seeming wealth of knowledge and mythology about physical experience that is accumulated in the first twenty years of life. Further it is enhanced by the impetuous yearning to demonstrate maturity. The physical juices are also beckoning. We have learned much, but not enough, in our early years from experience, family, and formative education in grades one to twelve. The dedication to sedentary study creates common problems, but some students seem born to that creative solitude. I don't believe I was made for that solitude even if my talents would be served with it. I felt I wanted to be my self – activist in the world. I wanted that hands-on feeling that sometimes can't wait for completion of formal education. It is a common feeling – especially among males. It nagged at me. In some ways it won, but at some cost.

There developed an impatience to get on with adult life and that with a sort of bravado as a warrior going to battle to overcome the odds and defeat the foe despite council to restful peace and delay. Or maybe it was a thirst for exploration and adventure similar to the walks in the woods with Peanut during halcyon days at Union Hill. Perhaps it was both. In any event, there was also a yearning for companionship and immediate fulfillment. Mathematics and engineering just didn't meet the personal pressures and invitations to the world beyond the hallowed halls of learning. Even in personal distractions I highly respected advanced education. Nature gave me my sense of freedom. It was magnetic for me. It seemed irresistible.

Melody was my High School sweetheart. I met her through her brother Wade. He was also a wrestler and, even with physical limitations, ultimately attended the California School for the Deaf in Berkley, California. During the summer, 1973, before my senior year at Las Plumas, he would, on several occasions, invite me over to his home to swim in the family pool. We got on well. Melody was an attractive young lady and soon my interest drifted romantically towards her. By the end of the summer we were dating.

I began somewhat clumsily entering the world of romance. One particular date became the most embarrassing moment in my life. We decided to go to the local movie theater where there were only few people in attendance. Taking our seats, we watched the advertisements showing cartoonish bags of popcorn and soda pop prancing across the screen. Wanting to make a good impression, I felt it appropriate for me to go to the snack bar and purchase an adequate supply of treats. Returning with popcorn, sodas and bon-bon candies in hand; I became somewhat disoriented inside the dark theater. The feature was about to begin on the screen. With my eyes on the movie I navigated to a seat that I thought was next to Melody. After appropriately placing the drinks and popcorn, I thought I would be cute to display my French sophistication impressing my date. Leaning close to her I said "Hey Baabby, want some bon-bons, hey?" It was then that horror struck when I realized this was not Melody but rather a strange and startled young lady unknown to me. Scanning the dimmed theatre, I soon sighted Melody who was sitting two rows back holding a perplexed look about antics she had observed that embarrassed her. Desperately seeking cover, I quickly gathered the goodies and cowered my way back to the appropriate seat next to the appropriate young lady. My sophistication had died in the interim. I had hit on a stranger. The only way it could have been worse would be the screaming of the startled young lady. She remained aghast but silent.

Not deterred from my romantic goal, Melody and I continued to date through my senior year in High School. While I was alone at Point Loma, we corresponded through letters. Her missives were laced with perfume that permeated the mail boxes in the college lobby. Dorm mates easily caught olfactory evidence when I received a letter from her and would let me know with friendly mocking – made of affectionate comments and dramatic gestures. Even though a bit embarrassed, I took it in stride. It was great fun. Other students were in the throes of romance as well. I didn't detect that their letters were as aromatic as mine. I was the culprit of the perfume mystery in the college postal arena.

Following my freshman year at Point Loma College and during summer recess, Don Libby's mom, who worked in the California Parks and Recreation Department, aided me in finding a summer job there. My duties were to assist in clean-up and general maintenance - picking up trash and making sure bathrooms were stocked and cleaned. It was a welcome relief from working in a cubicle as a fry cook. I liked to be physically active even if it had to include mundane chores. Living at home with no board and room costs I was able to save money for school and purchase my first car - a 1969 Toyota Corona with mag wheels. The wheels would scrape a bit on the side fenders whenever passing over an uneven surface. What was really important was that the car looked cool. It was mine, and another factor measuring adulthood, and active personal life.

During the summer, Melody and I were together during most of the hours off the job. Either we were swimming in her home pool, frequenting the movie theatre or going on family outings. It was all fun stuff for us, fitting to our ideals and years. Our families became good friends and we had become quite attached to each other which made it difficult to leave and return to college for sophomore studies. During the sophomore semester I made once a month trips from San Diego to Oroville in the trusty Toyota. (I still think it was cool!) By the end of the fall semester, 1975, I decided it would be better for me to go home and finish my education at Chico State. The call of my home situation was strong, with Melody the crowning attraction. Looking back I don't know if it was the right decision, but it was made.

We live with the consequences of our decisions for good or ill. We rightly accept the responsibility for what we do as maturing persons. We can make well of our lives even if we stumble along the way. Our parents were against the move back home, but romantic love pressed its way. Life doesn't turn on our mistakes and omissions if we, in reasonable schedule, apply our gifts and fulfill responsibility - with the sense that God will guide us along. Most educators and family counselors would say that I should have remained and finished the course at Point Loma. I am grateful that whatever decision one makes in such situations God cares for us in different options if we follow in life meaning to serve the needs of mankind. Almost all persons encounter detours, but they can find the way back to the highway. For me everything didn't turn on geography. I do not want to degrade my decisions nor my emerging experience. We do travel different highways. That's human life. Some stretches of the highway are in repair, even detoured. We ought to know there can be recovery from earlier uncertainties, but we do have to engage life at some reasonable point to find legitimate fulfillment. I did gain the advantage of cerebral life from my experience first at Point Loma, and later at Chico State – even though I did not follow through to the degree finals. At least I was taking responsibility for my decisions. I readily acknowledge that what college experience I had served me well.

Mom never voiced her opinion one way or the other but Dad was not in favor of my leaving Point Loma to go to Chico State and let it be known that he thought it was the wrong choice. Our differences over the matter were further compounded when I announced that Melody and I were going to get married during the upcoming summer. Dad remained staunch in his opinion and questioned my reasoning. He pointed out the obvious that she would still have one year remaining in high school and questioned the logistics of trying to attend college while trying to support a family. Both of us were stubborn in the exchanges and neither equipped with effective communication skills for such a family and life matter. Our relationship became severely strained. Our solidarity for a period was wounded. I am told that this is often common experience for emerging adults and their parents. With ambition to prove my independence and that combined with an attitude of some arrogance about my own independence, I found a small apartment in Oroville that had been converted from a motel. So to move from home the transition from my birth family was not as cordial as it should have been – also something of common tragedy for families. We need better preparation for learning how to merge from dependence to independence, to move from children to adults. We are often clumsy in making any transitions in our lives. But they will and must occur. Our problem is to learn how to make them with greater skill. What my family meant to me should never be lost, not even 'for a while.' But it was – 'for a while.' That winter and spring I enrolled at Chico State while working in what had become the dreaded coffee shop. Realizing that my father and my soon to be father-in-law were protesting our wedding plans, we decided to raise our own money for the wedding. We would win the generational conflict with financial independence in all matters. We were a bit bloodied, but unbowed. So it was during that summer, 1975, I worked two full time jobs. During the day I was at the Parks Department while working nights at the restaurant. Melody and I were able to save enough to have a nice ceremony. At least we were taking on responsibilities, so to counter family objections. The only solution really would be in taking on our hard won obligations in good spirit. So we launched – on our own. We were too innocent to know that romance doesn't hold for life solidarity and personal satisfaction. Dad finally accepted our decision to marry. He may have remembered his own history of debatable decisions or perhaps he recalled that he at age twenty, and Mom at sixteen, eloped because Mom's mother (my Grandmother) was adamant against it. However, Melody's father did not give in and demonstrated his disapproval by refusing to attend the wedding ceremony.

But that was the extent of his protest and he soon accepted me as his son-in-law. Family meant much to all of us, we couldn't fall out for long. We were on our way in gaining belated approval from our parents. Like most loving parents they found acceptance when inevitable events were settled. Melody at seventeen and me at twenty - we set up our home in the small apartment I had rented earlier. We soon discovered that the residence was too small, much too small, to accommodate two persons so we found a larger apartment in a duplex on the south side of town. We sensed even more in these little life amendments that we were on our way even if prematurely. The college thing was fading. Romance, an apartment, a cool Toyota and forgiving parents had won the day. It seemed better than college. No waiting.

As fall transitioned into winter, Coach Brown asked about my thoughts on starting a wrestling program at Palermo Unified School. The school consisted of kindergarten through 8th grade and was a major feeder school to Las Plumas High. His vision was to develop a program so that when kids arrived at the high school they would have some basic experience in the sport. I jumped at the opportunity and soon persuaded the school to purchase a wrestling mat. We even competed against big Central as well as other schools in Chico and Paradise. I worked as a budding Coach Brown. He was a model I admired. Many of the wrestlers from Palermo went on to High School and wrestling competition. They kept Las Plumas High as one of the top wrestling schools in the Section for some years. I feel rightly proud of the accomplishments with those child-students and often reflect fondly relative to my time there. My active role with students became part of my education missed by my earlier omissions or drop outs, but the preoccupation, though good was not in the area my tests indicated for life's professional success. Our emotions often leave off following our brains. There was some personal fulfillment in participation to form the lives of older children. One feels meaning and gratification in such involvement. But there had to be more. I needed a vision if I was to find something to complete formation of my life and family.

One day in the spring, 1979, the school's principal, Ken Staley, approached and encouraged me to obtain a license to drive in the school bus program. That way I could pick up students in the morning, go to college in Chico during the day and come back in the afternoon to drop the children off at their homes. Best of all, I could quit the coffee shop and its sporadic hours to focus on my college program at Chico. If all worked well I could complete the thirty units remaining to qualify for graduation in spring, 1980, with a BA degree in Mathematics. It appeared that I could return to my original and recommended academic objective. Out of the blue, I was being given another opportunity. Could I transition back to the halcyon days of college? Perhaps, as they say, "I could have my cake, and it eat it too."

What seems like the best design is sometimes thwarted, and we turn or are forced to turn in an alternate direction. Some might say: "It is God's will." However, if not careful we could blame the Divine as an excuse to make our own choices for direction and performance. God appears to aid us in our lives even when we change plans. His leading is always in the cooperative design with free persons. His concern is in the quality of our lives with flexibility to cover some of our uncertainties about our life steps and professions. He can make second or third choices work well when a devotional humility rises to aid repairs. There is an element of providence that permits life substitutions if we sustain faith. We are influenced in variant directions in our 'Pilgrim's Progress.' Philosophers, religious and secular, have debated and warred over philosophy about our life choices without agreed settlement on the answers. I know that it is above my pay grade to decide - better left for Deity. Each person bears his or her own responsibility. One of the best explanations I have heard is from the movie "Forrest Gump" in which Forrest is at the gravesite of Jenny and seeking answers to whether Lieutenant Dan's philosophy of destiny is correct or is it his, 'momma's belief of choice.' He comes to the conclusion; "Maybe it's both." Our lives are really corporate in the nature of the earth's system for the management of mankind. Sometimes I felt like I was on a see-saw – up and down.

I may have missed the understanding of the conflicts of thought and emotion.

After my first month of school restart and doing quite well in my classes, thinking I was on my way, we found that Melody was pregnant with our first son, Tyler. I was ecstatic that we were having a child but I also knew that there were related responsibilities coming up – added to those we currently bore. At the time we owned two vehicles; a 1974 Chevrolet Luv pickup and a 1976 Datsun B210. One day in early October, while on my way from Oroville to Chico, the timing chain on the Chevy broke and ripped out the housing along the front of the engine. A couple weeks later I noticed that the Datsun had oil in the radiator and there was water in the oil. The mechanic told me that the head on the Datsun was warped and the cost would be around $2,000 to repair while the Chevy would also be another $2,000. This was a huge amount of money for a poor college student especially when added $5,000 for college tuition annually. Finances were getting out-of-hand, and would likely worsen – what with a baby coming on. What to do? A wife and baby to care for, debts to pay, cars broken down, and dreams becoming muddled – what does a young man do? Barriers between me and higher education were increasing toward even higher barriers for life and lower expectations for higher education. Again, I was in the 'soup.'

Extrapolating from the long ago experience of The Accident, I realized I needed to accept the responsibilities and bear fully the burden of providing for my family. No one else had the responsibility. Even with the degree so near, I dropped out of college, gave my resignation to the Palermo School District on the bus driving and sought full time employment to pay for the repair of our vehicles and support our new addition. This was a severe transition – a challenge needing maturity and discipline to work through. It was the last opportunity to finish college for me.

You may have guessed it, I returned to the restaurant business at Jim's Coffee Shop where I worked the swing shift. It was not (as you may have detected) my favorite job, but it might meet the bills for my soon to be expanded family. I remembered the issues of family support from my parent's experience during poverty years. We had worked through lean times. I was determined to work through mine on my own, with my wife's help and adjustments. I felt like I was backpedaling, but I was determined to move forward.

Because finances were tight my father-in-law convinced me that I could repair the Chevy Luv myself. So with a Chilton manual in hand, I set out to delve into the world of mechanics. (Remember, I was supposed to be a genius in math and engineering.) I had no idea that it would require special tools such as torque wrenches and feeler gauges. Troubles ensued in my sincere attempt to 'do it myself.' Bolts were accidently sheared off, gaskets were improperly installed, and wrong parts were purchased. Oftentimes motors in the raw look different than they do on paper. Was I making matters worse? To set myself to repair that car was one of the worst decisions I ever made. However, it proved to be a meaningful learning experience - considering my limitations. It was a good education in understanding that I would be money ahead to take it to the experts and pay them to do their job. I determined that in order to engage the expert I needed to be an expert in something – so to afford the other experts. It was another one of those 'aha' experiences which offered transition. I have also been told that most persons gain 'aha' experiences and muffle them. We do get mixed up as the fellow who argued that we need to fire up our ambition – and water it. We mix our metaphors. When we pay attention, matters improve. Don't pour water on a fiery ambition.

The refreshed reality of supporting my own family made me realize that at least a third of my active life was going to be spent working and saving so it must be important for life meaning. I began an honest evaluation of my true personal gifts. In order to find them, I had to contemplate my interests and passions. I knew I did not want to be cooped up in a kitchen when I much preferred to be outside – in nature. I also knew that I had a proficiency in math and that I was curious about geographic information with a major propensity for history. Not knowing what would meet those criteria, I began a quest in searching with serious concern for the career fitting for me – one that would provide support for my family. As great as love is – you can't eat it or pay the rent with it. And – I wanted adequate meaning for my life, a meaning that I enjoyed.

Dad had quit his job with the California Division of Highways and started a trucking business transporting goods throughout the State. My brother Dean was with him in the venture. Since I had a license to drive a school bus, it seemed a logical choice to consider driving truck. It did give outdoors experience. At that point I was willing to do almost anything but cook in a restaurant for the rest of my life. Qualifying for my learners' permit for heavy trucking, I was permitted by Dad to drive the four hour shift from Oroville to a packing shed at the Oregon border. Even though it was good to be with Dad, I felt isolated in the cab from the rest of the world and could not adopt driving as a career. Driving is noble in meeting human needs, but it wasn't for me. That was a quickie transition – from nothing to nothing in my private world. Why did I always feel cooped up? My truck driving was short–lived – one trip.

During our only trip, Dad emphasized to me that I should be an engineer and work for the State of California. The idea intrigued me. In order to do that I had to go back to school, but the old bugaboo was still there - no funds to pay the way. He sympathized and the air was filled with the sense of regret for past choices but accentuated with awareness that we have to press forward and accept our responsibilities in a mature and reasonable way. We can influence our circumstances. There had to be another transition for me.

There was still time for me, but time was running out.

Some years later, after I became a surveyor, Dad pointed out that he told me I should be an engineer. When I responded that I was a surveyor and not an engineer, he retorted that either profession was the same thing. To a dedicated surveyor those can be fighting words, particularly to this surveyor. However, I took the exchange in stride with a tiny groan of protest. Dad was neither an engineer nor a surveyor. But he was still my Dad. We had gotten over tensions of disagreements about my life.

After that trip, Larry Tomlinson (who had funded my first college year at Point Loma) contacted me and asked me if I wanted to work for him in his mobile home business. My duties were to assist the four workers in their jobs by running for supplies, crawling under the homes to set blocks or bolt double wides together. I had no clue about what I was doing and discovered I do not have any natural handyman abilities. My gifts were somewhere on a shelf out there. I had not yet found my way professionally, but knew that I needed to. I was getting older, had a family to support, and felt a need to be better fulfilled. There seemed always to be jobs available, but they didn't fulfill my imagination.

However, I did learn the principles of electricity while on this job. On one occasion I was handling the jack by lifting the home up so as to insert blocks at the appropriate level. At the same time a fellow worker, Chuck, was attempting to wire the electric panel. Unknown to us was a short in the wiring system of the metal home. When Chuck switched the power on, it sent a current through the metal sheeting and into the handle of the jack I was using. It sent a jolt through my system. It took an hour or so for me to recover from both the physical shock and the disturbing thought that it could have been much worse. The matter made me more aware of life, meaning and work. This kind of experience may mature us more rapidly than formal education. Living is serious business. I was learning something from every job that would serve me, but fulfillment evaded me. My brain seemed to be scrambled.

Aside from Larry, the persons with whom I worked did not attend college, but their knowledge of practical engineering was exemplary. I was impressed. Using jacks, wenches, and 'come alongs' we maneuvered homes as a team through winding roads, around large boulders and thick vegetation to destinations without permitting a scratch on the product house. It was marvelous to behold – the work of mankind to a good end for the benefit of others, likely strangers. When a rightly functioning team works well it becomes relational dignifying human beings. We were meant to serve together in such relationships – as families or between nations. It helps us to sense who we are, and learning that even in labor we use humility for interdependence. There is no room for arrogance. It is not easy to dislike someone you have helped – or helps you.

On one occasion I was stretched out underneath a home setting blocks as streams of rain water flowed around me. With my clothes soaked and caked with mud, I crawled out from underneath the home. My appearance gained the supervisor's attention related to the deplorable weather conditions for our assignment. Al, who was a retired Air Force sergeant, laughed and told me I wouldn't melt and that the buyers were depending on us to complete our task so they could get out of the rain. Realizing the importance of what we were doing, I crawled back under the structure with a service purpose in mind. Someone was relying on me to do a job, and I would do it. I felt good about myself – mud and all. It was another 'aha' experience. It is good to be needed. It is better to serve. I am told that even our health quotients may be affected favorably if we feel others need us. I like knowing that I am serving a human need – or that of an animal. The point is to have the heart of a servant to others in a context of respect. I believe that is what God could have me be and do.

Oftentimes I assisted Vern, who was from West Virginia and conversed with a creative and heavy mountain accent. One day I wandered into the supply shed and found Vern looking through metal strips for trimming doors. I asked if I could help him and he responded he was looking for a, "Narr one." To me it appeared that 'Narr' was either a type of metal or a brand name. After several minutes of proceeding to be helpful, acting like I knew what a 'Narr' strip looked like, I concluded that my endeavor was futile wasting time. So I asked Vern what a 'Narr' strip looked like. He answered, " Narr! " holding his hand up and illustrating a narrow (Narr) distance between his thumb and fore-finger. The proverbial lights went on as I realized Narr was West Virginian for narrow. Our lives are commonly touched with these vignettes that teach us the range of differences between persons. We learn acceptance and appreciation for others – sometimes greater respect in the dedication to the little necessaries of life. Vern was hard at work. I respected that then as I do now.

All these odd jobs didn't appeal to me, but I liked the people I worked with and learned from them. I was going somewhere, I did not know where but wherever it was these men contributed to the destination. I owe to them a tip of the hat, which is a sincere salute, of appreciation for their contributions to my life. It took a few years for me to appreciate fully that all this contributed to maturation. It is also great to know that Scripture refers to maturation as moving in God's direction. Daily experience is important to the making of life when we draw from it – for good or ill. It is up to us not up to the experience. Knowing that I to have a hand in choosing my experiences is reassuring. Only a little of life is accidental. We can make that useful too. Remember 'the Accident.'

I worked about six months for Larry and learned about proper work ethics, engineering and even voice dialects. I enjoyed working outside and likely would have worked longer for him but it became apparent that I was not the most mechanically inclined person on the team. So when it came time for layoffs in April, 1980, I was the first employee to go. Larry called me up to the porch of the office and informed me that unfortunately he had to let me go because there was not enough work to continue the present team in its full number. He sympathized that my first born was only a month away from birth but there was nothing he could do because of the current slump in the business situation. He also suggested that he knew that my former employer, Jim's Coffee Shop, needed a cook to work the evening shifts. We talked about family responsibilities and doing what needed to be done to support them. There was encouragement in his words as he told me that even though I hated working in a restaurant that I would find the career that suited me. You guessed it again - Jim's Coffee Shop loomed as my rescue. (Any port will do in a storm.)

I reluctantly went back to Jim's - discouraged, thinking I was being trapped in a career that was beyond my voluntary control and far short of my interests. However, my discouragement soon eased to joy when in May, our Tyler was born. I was so proud of being a father that I had a T-shirt tailored that served as a billboard: "Ask me about my son, Tyler." Nineteen years later I decided to wear that same shirt, much to the embarrassment of my son, at his going-away party before leaving home for the Air Force. By then I had put on a few pounds and the shirt did not quite reach my belt thus exposing a bit of my dun-lop disease of forty four years. (That is when the abdomen dun-lopped over the belt buckle.) Everyone thought it was hilarious - except Tyler. So for his comfort I changed to something a little more appropriate, and much more sophisticated. I had accomplished my comedy purpose. Great fun!

Our new addition created the inevitable shifting in family life style, but there was another change in May, 1980, that would set me on a course that offered hoped-for professional satisfaction and the sense of worth I was seeking. It was a change that would woo me to a life of new experiences, mysteries and adventures; to a career that was calling me for my life's work; to a profession that would assist me in understanding my duty to myself, family, and society; and, I believe, to God. The few years of educational and non-directional professional wandering were about over. I finally experienced the transition that I longed for. However, that too would take some maturing to gain life satisfaction.

I was about to make a great career choice for my life. I had passed through small doors of this or that job, I was about to find the light of my professional life just beyond the gate of a meaningful life transition. It wasn't a 'narr' one.

*Mom and Dad celebrating their 25ᵗʰ Wedding Anniversary with friends and family. Eleven years after "The Accident."*

# 8
# Stakes for Steaks

*"Anybody for Rattlesnake Meat?"*
Grubb

Following my discussion with Larry concerning my layoff, I went home to share the bad news with Melody. She seemed aloof to the situation and more preoccupied with the imminent birth of our first child. This deepened my prevailing feeling, bordering on depression that I might fail in carrying my family responsibilities. My dreams and ambitions of contributing to family and society in a meaningful profession perhaps in teaching were scrambled, perhaps dashed. The thought of going back with hat-in-hand seeking again for a job at the restaurant; but that raised in me a feeling of being emasculated. For the most part the culinary portion of the job was enjoyable. However, the odd hours and the constraints of being inside a warm room for continuous hours were overwhelming. I was less than enthusiastic about returning. Further, the pay scale wasn't adequate for needs of a growing family. There was pause in my professional hopes. Was I ever going to break out?

During the short stint of laboring for Larry at the mobile home business, I grew accustomed to working daylight hours as well as having weekends and holidays free from work duty. In restaurant business, the peak hours are mornings, evenings and weekends. Holidays such as Memorial Day, Fourth of July and Labor Day encourages outdoor home BBQ for lunch and dinners, but not for daily breakfasts, or late meals in the day brings. My shift got the heaviest duty. Work days ran late. During busy hours customer requests often became overwhelming. Diners usually did not come in as individuals or parties of two but rather with family and friends of six or more on their way to Lake Oroville for a day of fun in the sun. It was not uncommon to have a dozen or more of these groups at one time all jockeying to get their meals so that they could get to leisure destinations. Attempting to accommodate them could be a severe trial, even helter-skelter to assure that every person in respective groups received their orders at the same time. Service often became a difficult balancing act. Those who had oatmeal wanted to eat at the same time as those ordering steak and eggs. We truly wanted to serve, but the challenge could be overwhelming, and excessive under pressure. We tried. Diner demands came with the job. However, it all took some negative toll on employees. The greatest love for me was on my marriage and I didn't catch it.

Inside the restaurant, at the cook's station, I found myself observing the outside world through the restraint of an opening in the wall measuring two by six feet. Placing the plates of food through this portal and calling: "Order Up" - to the waitress, I would catch a glimpse of the outdoors and then let out a sigh - or it may have been a moan. Peering through the opening and past yonder window I could see a landscape of trees that waved in unison with gentle breezes as if motioning for me to join them. I resisted the alluring temptation during such imaginations as escape from a box of solitary confinement. I returned to reality - reminding myself of responsibilities to my family. Press on! Press on! Press on! In all, it didn't create a longing to start my own restaurant business. I was meant to serve in some other professional context. This context was not meant for me.

During the Christmas season, the evenings were filled with a seemingly endless parade of hungry shoppers desiring the necessary nourishment for the sole purpose of continuing the day in their happy ventures. There was also the Bar crowd. They thought of the season as a time to party, even late into the night. They would come in after their excursions seeking food and coffee to counter alcohol tipsy. I wanted to do something more with my life than comfort revelers. I wonder, and sometimes feel awed, about those who do find the effort worthy of their time. It wasn't for me. I knew there was something else for me. Something worthy of life and meaning, as I understand the matter.

Going back to the restaurant business meant working during those long hours. Sometimes I was forlorn in spirit. More importantly it robbed me of quality time with my wife and our new son. While they were sleeping I would be working and while I was sleeping they would be awake. Family outings were limited in that oftentimes I would not have successive days off. For example, I might be off Monday, work Tuesday, off Wednesday, then work Thursday through Sunday. Even then, I might be called in to work on those off-days because either an employee was ill or didn't show up for duty. The restaurant business employs many persons casual with their time perceptions. It was difficult to plan trips further than the confines of Oroville, only a few miles up the pike. Going on a Date Night was next to impossible because there was not much to do with others on Mondays and Wednesdays. I felt somewhat bereft, and my family forced to take second place.

Sometimes there were pleasant diversions; Tuesday was a bit of a bright spot in that it was: All you can eat Liver & Onions night. I feel compelled to admit, in my moderate humility, my specialty of Liver & Onions as the best anywhere – at least on the Tuesdays I worked. We had quite a few regulars who would come in, order Liver & Onions, tip me anywhere from one to five dollars for their meals, and, even leave me notes of appreciation. The secret recipe (now freely offered at no cost to my reader) was to marinate the liver in milk for at least 2 hours then sauté in butter at a low temperature. Most people rush the process making the liver look and taste likes burnt cardboard with onions that are under cooked. If prepared correctly, the delicacy is a savory blend that melts in the mouth. (As already noted there is no charge for my recipe of the heavenly ambrosia listed above. A financial gift to any creative chef found here or there will be greatly appreciated as proper gratuity award.)

My view at the time was that the restaurant business, particularly as a fry cook, was a dead end job. (My apologies to fry cooks for my personal concern for those who serve so well in restrictive environments.) Unless one aspires to gain Chef Status, which requires culinary school, the pay is, or was at the time, only a little more than minimum wage. Later in life I have come to realize that the restaurant business can be rewarding if one likes food preparation and gains professional training it – and does not mind to being cooped up inside a warm bustling kitchen. It is an artistic profession. But for me it was repulsive to think of the endless parade of different scents of cuisine clogging the nostrils and the slimy coating of grease on the skin. It was so prevalent in my circumstances that when I arrived home, Sam, the family dog did not leap up to greet me, but rather began licking, and inhaling, the residues on my shoes. All this aroused the traumatic consideration simmering inside me that suggested the sensation of a kind of undeserved imprisonment. I wasn't given a choice. Responsibilities to my family again outweighed slothful behavior of not engaging in the expansive labor force, so I went back to the cell. Ugh! Others must judge if this was good or ill fortune. At least I was mature enough to accept duty. The Coffee Shop did serve as a port in the storm – several times. I must be grateful for that – and I do feel gratitude for the challenges to meet responsibility. Sometimes duty plays odd roles with our preferences.

Tyler was born in early May, 1980, and I was the proudest man on the planet. His presence caused me to feel deeply that I had been entrusted with the welfare of his life. It was another 'aha' experience moving me toward adult maturity. Melody began birth labor around 10 o'clock the night before and delivered around 6am the next morning. It was tough going; but with great reward. Before Tyler was born we didn't know if he was going to be a boy or girl but when he arrived I took away the doctor's usual announcement by thundering: "It's a boy!" By those words I would bring him from whatever "It" means to humanity. To say, "He's a boy" - seems redundant, and obvious.

Even though I had been up all night, I was flying high all day and handed out suckers to everyone I met that day. To a few special people, I gave bubble gum in the shape of a cigar. (I didn't know more than a couple of people who smoked tobacco cigars.) My kind could be eaten without any health concern - except to rejoice with me. That evening I played in a softball game where I enjoyed the game of my life. I hit for the cycle (single, double, triple and homerun) and made several spectacular catches. My teammates wanted Melody to have a baby before every game. (For us – that is highly unlikely.) Life was looking good, even for a fry cook. I just needed a career that would offer stability and provide necessities my family deserved, and I deeply wanted to provide.

One Friday evening in late May, 1980, our church softball team was involved in a playoff game. I was able to switch hours with another cook so that I could participate. Before the game I was playing catch with my good friend Jerry Unfried, who had attended Point Loma College with me. He told me that he had been offered a summer position working for the U.S. Forest Service surveying roads for timber sales. He added that he was not going to take the position because he found another job managing a restaurant in Chico. (Good for him.) So we conjured a plan that he would go in at 9am on Monday and inform the manager of his decision, and then shortly after he would depart I would casually go in asking for a job. It worked. I was hired later that day.

With little cognizance of land surveying, I asked Jerry for the job description. He explained that it would entail walking down trails and measuring the best route for a logging road which might require clearing ground brush. I did not want to spend the summer doing yard work, but I did not want to work inside a greasy restaurant either. So the decision was to submit my application on Monday and wait to see what might happen. If this didn't work out I could always go back to the restaurant. (Another, Ugh.) The restaurant was always there, and the owners seemed to need me whenever I needed them. They were always there in my time of need.

On Monday at 9:30 I drove to the Forest Service office and asked the clerk if there were any openings. I completed an application and left. Shortly thereafter I received a call from the Forest Service asking me if I wanted to fill a position that just opened up. If I wanted the job I would need to come back down that day and complete additional paper work. With the job starting on the following Monday, they needed time to process my clearance to work for the government. (The whole event is evidence of the highly regarded concept of networking to gain employment or gain a cause – the plan of Unfried and Nelms.)

If all went well I would be stationed in a small mountain community about 50 miles east of Oroville dubbed La Porte where the work would consist of four 10 hour days Monday through Thursday. This sounded very good - to have three day weekends. The only problem was that the Forest Service only provided transportation to La Porte on Monday morning and transportation back on Thursday evening. That required staying over for three nights, leaving Melody alone with our new born, unless I wanted, at my own expense, to drive my personal vehicle back and forth Monday through Wednesday nights. Because it was cost prohibitive, Melody acquiesced to the idea of me staying in La Porte during the nights on the job. Tyler would now have our week ends together.

I arrived at the office in Oroville at six in the morning with an ice chest of food, a suitcase, and no idea of what a surveyor does. My companion employees were easy to spot. Who else would be up at this hour? The group consisted of three field crews with five persons in each crew. I was assigned to a soft spoken portly man and informed that he was my: "Party Chief." Identifying his position in this way caused me to have visions of fun and frolic, but I soon found out that the title (Party) was more in the realm of participating on a team with each responsible for a specific task. Party doesn't really sound masculine for energetic work encountered in this business of measuring the earth's surface for the use of huge trucks. But, Party it was. ("Team" would have been better.)

The camp in La Porte consisted of three bunk houses. Each slept four men - complete with a shower facility. A fourth building accommodated three and included a fully equipped kitchen. We were informed that we would have to prepare our own meals and clean up after ourselves. Not wanting to spend time in the kitchen cooking, washing my dishes, and hiding my unwanted cooking skills, I chose with the others to go with TV dinners and food in Tupperware brought from home that could be reheated. My staple of choice was either frozen pot pies or sandwiches. In this no one could detect my chef credentials. I felt no obligation to discuss my life history or brag about liver and onions.

Nestled between the buildings was a picnic area with tables and an open fire pit. It served as a gathering place both at the beginning and ending of our work days. The camp site also consisted of a dirt volleyball court in which some of us would play at the end of the day - so to create welcome entertainment. Even though the games were often attended with spirited competition, it didn't seem to quite come up to wrestling as a manly sport. Besides – we were tired after ten hours in the field.

Our first day consisted of orientation of the campsite and instructions of our duties. It provided practical schooling. Academia offers theories and formulas but sometimes it lacks in explaining their relevance and importance to everyday life. During those few hours with the three Party Chiefs and two persons on the crew who had worked the woods during previous summers, I began to comprehend the practical uses of mathematics, more particularly geometry and trigonometry. Before that morning, those subjects meant little more than recreational games for me similar to a crossword puzzle. I was considered adept with the concepts in the classroom, but here I could really use them practically. I liked that. To take learnings from classroom to work space was a pleasant transition for me. Learning became doing. It is not only a human principle but spiritual. The context causes something to happen within the mind-soul relating to self - meaning. I felt it. I practiced to make it fit my assignments. I liked all of it.

The first tool handed to me was a handheld compass measuring 2 square inches and ½ inch deep with a 'peep' hole in the gadget. During my brief stint with the Boy Scouts as a lad, I was introduced to a hand held magnetic compass and briefly taught how to read it. The Scout leader showed me an instrument that determined directions - by means of a freely rotating needle that indicated magnetic north. This new compass was circular and separated into four quadrants: northeast, southeast, southwest, and northwest. In high school geometry I had learned that a circle has 360 degrees and therefore each quadrant has 90 degrees. Even as a lad I was on my way through the gate of my preferred opportunity. I was learning about what I was about to do. The practicality appealed to me. The application appeared to be creative. With Math an easy factor for me, I was immediately: "On my way."

However, the compass handed to me was different from the standard compass I used in the Scouts in that it measured the Azimuth instead of the aforementioned quadrants. The party chief explained to me that an azimuth is the horizontal angle of a bearing clockwise from North. How about that? For example 0 degrees would be north, 90 degrees equates to East, while 180 degrees is south and 270 degrees measures west. This made it simpler to add and subtract the courses of lines to acquire the needed angle. Our goal was to find a manageable angle for a road so to make transport possible and preserve the landscape. This angle coupled with the distances could then be calculated to determine the location of the desired points from each other. Of a sudden I had an epiphany as I realized the math I took in high school and college had relevance in the real world. (Another aha!) It really does work – and is necessary for modern ordered society. I don't recall that I heard angels singing or lights shining from heaven, but all the same it was an enlightening moment and exciting. Something was happening – and happening fast within my mind and spirit. It felt good. Was I finally going to enjoy my work? At the moment, my work seemed to be fitted exactly to my life. Or was my life fitted to the needed skills. For me they were the same.

The second tool handed to me was a clinometer. This tool was the same size as the compass except it assisted in measuring the percentage slope of a specified line. They informed me that instead of horizontal it assisted in measuring vertical angles. This is significant in determining a steady slope that will transition fluently for vehicular travel, in this case logging trucks. Again, the mathematical formulas further were evolving for me into their importance for the real world.

The amateur Mathematician will have to trust me. It works – seeming like a miracle when carefully done. No wonder the academicians liked Math – even when some of them were still counting on their fingers

We were also given lessons on the proper use of a "Swede Ax." This ax consisted of a wood handle three feet in length with a metal 'C' shape blade on the top end. Running along the tips of the "C" was a thin sharp blade of about 6 inches long and one inch wide. Its purpose is to assist in clearing small limbs and brush in order to obtain a line of sight. We were told that when not in use it should be in a leather scabbard to prevent injury to self and others. My previous negatives about doing yard work were abated in understanding that this trimming was for the sole purpose of surveying and not for manicured aesthetics. Something needed by mankind for orderly life was worth my time to clear away the undergrowth. It was simple and ordinary procedure, seemingly mundane and ordinary – like being a fry cook. Grass length on a lawn didn't qualify for me. Here was the burly life – fit for a wrestler. Life was already getting better even though I wasn't in mature practice yet. I could hardly wait for tomorrow. Here I was finding work that combined physical with cerebral activity. I was feeling better by the hour.

The second day our crew of five men loaded into the suburban and travelled several miles through forested lands thick with grand cedar, fur, and pines. Along the way, we engaged several creeks flowing over and around boulders even through some vegetation. Other flows meandered into lush green meadows. Majestic mountain peaks towered above us. Deep canyons beckoned in a silent call. Beautiful rock formations drew attention as did the eagles that soared over us. This was like an Eden to me. Something was calling to me even in some silence, but accompanied by the background sounds of nature. Sure beats the environment for hash slingers.

Eventually we came to the beginning of a marked trail which was identified by a short stake (lath) with writing that I did not understand. Standing at the stake we could peer into the forest and see a line of little flags tied to limbs, bushes, and trees. Who marked this line was a curiosity to me but I deduced that it must have been placed by some official high up in the government as a proposed route for a logging road. My deduction turned out to be a true one.

We established the starting point at the center of the existing road opposite the short stake and marked it station 1+00. So we knew where we were and where we were supposed to be. Now we had to map where we wanted the trucks to go. Without our work well done the future plan for product could not be carried through. It had to be done, and done right. I was told we never start at 0+00 in case we have to move our starting point backwards which would create a negative station. One of the experienced hands tied the end of three cloth tapes 100 feet long to his belt buckle. The purpose of this was to keep his hands free so he could operate the clinometer and compass while standing over the desired point. There was something of a symphony to it all.

The other experienced hand took one of the tapes and moved down the trail 100 feet, set a lath with his hammer and marked it station 2+00. Both of them then used their compasses so to give the azimuths both forward and back to the party chief who recorded it in the field notes. The purpose of this was to measure the existing conditions on the ground so that a roadway could be designed at the proper angles and slopes so that the heavy machinery needed to design surface for maneuvering easily through the forest. It was a creative work to be repeated several times during the day. The day didn't seem long – only 10 hours. They flew for me.

I stood on the side waiting for instructions. The party chief told me to stand next to the tape holder and level the clinometer until it read zero percent and then note the body part on his person. Since he was taller than I, it was the tip of his chin. This was done with the idea that the distance from my eyes to the ground would be the same as from his chin to the ground. That way the ground slope between us would be the same as the slope between my eyes to his chin as long as neither one of us slouched or stood on our toes. (Later in my professional years I learned that this was a an old somewhat crude way of measuring but it sufficed for the purposes of logging roads that did not need the same precision as public streets or great Interstates.) Even so, it was quite good when we stayed with the measurement of everything - even the height of crew members. You do remember that 2 plus 2 equals 4 – if you are measuring the same things. That is to say 2 pencils and 2 pencils equal 4 pencils, but 2 pencils plus 2 wrenches do not equal 4 pencils. It is good to know that 2 + 2 does not mean 4.

I was learning the value of precision. I was told to depart at 90 degrees to the trail and stop at any change of slope and use the clinometer by reading the percentage slope from my eyes to the Man's chin. I was then to shout out the slope indicated on the clinometer and the distance on the tape being sure to add one foot. The party chief then recorded this information and when complete we would move forward 100 feet to the next station (station 2+00) to repeat the process. Ultimately this would provide the map for the road builders.

For the first few weeks we weren't highly productive because of the learning curve for a few of us but by the end of the season we were able to survey about a half mile a day. This of course depended upon the terrain and impeding vegetation. It was a worthy effort. It was progressive and necessary to large future programming. And – it was all out-of-doors. It was creative.

Later I learned that what we were doing was profiling and cross sectioning a proposed road for a timber sale. They needed to know this information so that it could be designed and completed properly related to specific purpose – the transport of timber. By Thursday evening on my way home, I noticed the road we traversed was filled with slope changes. It was something I had never noticed before. A whole new geometric world began to open up, and I embraced it. Aha! This was my Eden.

One of the members on the team who assisted me in understanding this new world was a fellow by the name of Johnny Grubb. He was a student at Humboldt State University majoring in forestry. In fact and practice, he seemed to invite people to think of him as 'Grubby.' He effectively acted out the name in some of his antics. One evening he came back from the field with a rattlesnake that he had killed earlier and announced that he was going to prepare delectable reptile meat for human consumption. He inquired if anyone wanted to share in his triumph. No takers. All declined including me. I felt a bit queasy about Grubb's grubby ways, especially in food preparation. Fry cooks seemed suddenly to be quite sophisticated and more than merely acceptable for my taste. Snake meat, I am told is very tasty, but Grubb as a chef did not persuade me.

Because of my culinary background, curiosity got the best of me, so I wandered to the kitchen to find out how he prepared snake meat – a common dish for many outdoorsmen. My thoughts were that he was going to cook this delicacy in some sauce but that was not the case. He coiled the reptile on a baking sheet in the oven and cooked it at 375 degrees. When I arrived, he had the slender body spanned across the kitchen table, and the skeletal chain appealing after meat portion (that he had devoured) was dangling over the table edge – not a palatable sight. He was eating in serial fashion along the skeleton, the edible meat baked and untreated – an unforgivable sin to even a coffee shop cook. I could survive the event – an educated chef would have fainted away. Grubb's college education seemed different than mine. He may have picked up some manners before his graduation – which occurred after my time in the forest with him.

On another occasion Grubb came back from the field with a jack rabbit for his meal. Witnesses verified that the rabbit was startled from a bush and took off in a sprint, while Grubb not missing a beat, threw a Swede ax and hit the prey behind an ear from a distance of 25 feet. It was an incredible stroke of accuracy. He also prepared this creature for his consumption with little more seasoning than salt and pepper. It was another violation of the culinary art of preparing food. It was also reason enough for Grubby to dine alone. Which he did. (I wonder if he still does.)

There was no doubt about it, Grubb was a true outdoorsman and could survive in any situation. However, he had a nemesis which periodically gave him stinging reminders of their presence and disregard for his comfort. Meat bees are not really bees but belong to wasp strains. They mainly feed on insects and are scavengers of dead carcasses. They will colonize in large hives and attack as a unit if provoked. Their main arsenal is to bite and sting their victims simultaneously. These bees held a deep hatred for Grubb proving their emotions in that they would go for him when disturbed by any man in the crew. There was no affection returned by Grubb for the adoration of the bees. If he saw a hive he would try to destroy it. Nobody is sure how the feud was started but rumors have it that the bees tried to steal one of his kills, originally designated for one of his unprofessional culinary events that seemed tragic to me but a feast for him.

One day I had the privilege of working with Grubb. We were surveying the centerline of a proposed logging road in a tangled brushy area. On this particular day I was going down the cross slope while the middle person was measuring forward to Grubb. We had just started to separate and start our readings, when not more than five feet away, the person going up slope fell into a meat bee hive. He immediately rolled over and entangled the 100 foot tape line around himself and the brush; thus leaving the middle person on a leash from which he could not break free. On the crash into the hive, I and the party chief fled from the disaster as did Grubb, who was 100 feet away from us. The bees formed into a cloud and the unit passed all of us to make a bee line straight for Grubb. Although fleeing as fast as he could, the vengeful bees caught up with poor Grubby – punishing him for the treatment he gave to their ancestors. For his guilty past he became an unhappy recipient of a half dozen severe welts. No other crew member received a sting from the offended varmints. I do not know where Grubb may be found these days but my fantasy is that he is somewhere on the front lines battling his nemesis, and baking snake meat. I would change my mind about dining at a restaurant if I spied him in the kitchen of the establishment.

After a few months of experience the chief trusted me to be the middle man and read the azimuth and the slope. It was a real promotion. The good was getting even better. The proper procedure was to hold the compass in front of the mid-man and line up the compass with the person in front. This new assignment is when I found out that my left eye dominated my right because I kept reading a 2 degree difference from the front man. Because of my natural handicap I would have to position myself in a manner in which I had to look over my left shoulder while closing my right eye. (The problem may have descended to me - a physical trait inherited from my father's side of the family.) The adjustment required an artistic skill that would affect accuracy – unless I could make adjustments. I quickly adapted. I was in my element. Nothing would keep me out. I yearned for accuracy.

Another factor of which a crew member needed to be aware was local attraction. If there was iron in the area it would cause a distracted reading. Usually this only affected a reading by a degree or two and was discovered when the front reading did not match the back reading. I learned that it wasn't until the 1820s that surveyors became aware that magnetic compasses were susceptible to this phenomenon. That explains why there are so many problems with early surveys, particularly in the eastern United States – problems that are difficult to correct what with variant claims of land owners. It is likely that some of George Washington's readings in the Ohio Valley were off a bit for this reason. All things considered, our early map makers did fairly well without the equipment for accuracy we now enjoy. We continue to seek accuracy and attempt to correct errors of the past. Correction is not easy to do when a land owner discovers that ten feet of his lot line is closer to his house than that he was led to believe when he bought it. Further, one wonders if Washington's experience as surveyor served him well as a General and President. His skill leading men on foot in nature in all kinds of weather suggest that his early experience was a teacher. It may have saved lives for our side.

It was during these outings in the wilderness that I, a lover of nature, was privileged to view magnificent scenery and my experience in it remains in preferred memory. The experiences included, encounters with wild animals - bears, deer, eagles, owls, and even rattlesnakes at lengths up to six feet from head to rattle. I appreciate the magnificence of nature. It seems like my home. I invite my readers in. There is room for all of us. God made it and all living things in it for our sustenance and pleasure.

For six months I was employed by the Forest Service and learned about the fulfilling occupation and the world of Land Surveying. It was another aha experience, engaging my interests in the practical application of mathematics and my love for nature. I realized that I appreciated nature adventures to the full – including the practical mysteries to be engaged for human benefit. Land surveying was the perfect fit for me and so began a long sought career. I had found my way. The transitions to professional life had finally ended my professional search for the 'promised land.' Perhaps I poked around sufficiently long to find surveying. We rightly spend much of our time in search of ourselves. Some persons have a smoother journey of search than others and some never find it. The hours given to steaks as a cook in a cubicle gave way to stakes in the soil as a surveyor in nature. The restaurant business would, from this point forward, have to get along as best it could without me. It seems to have done well in the years since my rejection. I feel some relief in that survival. I had my part – especially with liver and onions. Further, I now know why our first president, Washington, was such a great leader, He was a Surveyor.

*Wrestling team from Palermo Elementary. A great group of kids who were enthused to participate despite not having uniforms. We were a bit rag tag but had a lot of fun.*

## 9
# *Uncovering Hidden Treasure*

*"He must recognize his inaccuracies, and govern his actions by facts."*
*Chief Justice Cooley*

By early September, 1980, most of my comrades at the Forest Service went back to pursue scholastic goals earning college degrees. I decided to stay on until the end of October. That is when I completed the fully allotted hours so to qualify and be considered seasonal related to official employment. Because I needed several years of experience, I was unqualified to work in the department full time. So that meant I would have to reapply the following spring and then wait until the snow melted in May. In the meantime I would be out of work. My wonderful summer was coming to the end. What about my future in the kitchen. (Don't, dear reader, even think the words: (fry cook.)

November arrived along with awareness of the approaching holiday season and the pressure of supplying not only family sustenance but all the extras that come with the holiday period of the year. Unlike my despondency over my layoff from the mobile home business, I now felt a skip in my step to find employment in this new found profession - land surveying. After all, I had almost six months of proficiency on a mixed résumé. Still young in years, I felt I belonged to society now – not just floundering about and wishing. My confidence was rising, with an affirmative spirit.

I had accumulated enough time to qualify for unemployment insurance while I was in the woods. Also, Melody found work at the County of Butte doing clerical work. So we decided that I would not have to go back to the restaurant business but instead make it my everyday job to find work as a surveyor. Our plan was that I had 6 months to find my way. I had to get cracking. Together with her work and my seasonal employment with the Forest Service, I felt determined.

The combination qualified us for a low income loan to purchase our first home. It was a three bedroom, two bath house a few miles west of Oroville in a community known as Thermalito. Our new home was only a few miles from my father-in-law's home. Since he was retired, he volunteered to watch Tyler during the day while we were so active about our professional goals. He dubbed him "Timmy Tyler" for some reason. His gracious offer allowed me to search for work and saved us the costs of babysitters. We seemed to be a family for generations, lifting the load for each other – just what families are meant to be – with members helping in the needs of those in life formation.

In those days before the Internet and Smart Phones, we used the Yellow Pages in the phone book to find businesses. My first order was to search those pages for engineering and land surveying firms in Oroville. At the time there were three and I made a phone call to each one to discover if they were hiring. One gave me a tentative response - GDA Engineering. I was invited to drop off a résumé. I had never been asked for a résumé. Before my quest to become a land surveyor, all my other job inquiries simply required completing an application provided by the potential employer. A résumé meant I would have to personalize my request instead of the usual forms where I filled out my name, address, and phone number. For GDA it wasn't a check list but rather they wanted answers for: why would I be a good asset for them? I had to become professional. The job was made important. Not just anybody could fill it.

Because my handwriting skills are scribbly and desiring to rise above the former norm, I pulled out my old typewriter and began to assemble my résumé. Some readers will remember that before the home computer there were typewriters, as covered wagons preceded the automobile. The use of these machines could be tedious if mistakes were made. Instead of simply back spacing or deleting with a touch of a key correcting the computer screen, one would have to brush the error with liquid white out and then wait for it to dry to retype. Even then the script might look patched. More sophisticated machines had white ribbon that necessitated holding down the appropriate key and the offending letter at the same time. However, these corrections could become easily noticeable and unacceptable. The typist would toss the paper away and start all over again. By current standards the process was lengthy, but I was determined to be professional.

Fortunately, I had taken a typing class during a summer recess in High School in which I got up to fifty words a minute. It turned out to be the most practical class I could have taken and I highly recommend it instead of the two finger hunt and peck that many use. Of course with texting today it has more to do with the thumbs than the fingers. For me when seeing the little key board on my phone, I feel compelled to place both hands on it which of course is awkward and impractical. Such is life, but the balanced person laughs off the oddities and goes for the goal. It doesn't take long to become a backward person in society. It is good to adapt to progress. Even ol' folks can do it -If they try hard enough. The experience was meaningful to lifting the quality of my life's work. I hate excuses for myself.

With my modest résumé laboriously assembled and realizing a need to broaden my search for other potential employers, I decided that duplicates were necessary. However, during those days copy machines weren't prevalent so if you wanted a copy you either went to the library or the local super market where for 25 cents you could get a page or two done. You could use carbon paper, but that was sloppy – some other person was receiving an original – the better copy. The copy was 'second rate.' The cost would be equivalent to about $1.20 by today's money values. Often-times the customer was delayed as the machine would not be working – likely in need of repair. If they were functioning, the quality was often so poor that one would not use it. So desiring to save finances and to maintain quality, I decided to retype the résumé several times instead of spending money on unreliable machines. I really wanted it to look professional. It took some days to get the simple job done with fresh copies for every interview. (Still, it was better than fry cooking.) The systems we used just three decades ago now seem antiquated. They are!

My next step was to go to each of the three firms in Oroville and personally hand them my carefully cast résumé. At each one I was only permitted to give it to the receptionist but I asked if the company was hiring. The responses were the same from each receptionist. They weren't 'sure' but would give my first class résumé to the appropriate officer. Not discouraged, I decided to expand my search to the nearby city of Chico where there were a half a dozen firms.

Later I moved on to other neighboring cities of Paradise, Marysville, and Yuba City. But it was 1980 and the nation was in the middle of a recession caused by runaway inflation. Some bank rates for standard loans ran 15%. Annuities were paying over 12%. Work was not to be found until GDA Engineering contacted me in early December for an interview. All that searching and renewed tenacity for typing excellence that might pay off. Hope is eternal.

Arriving at the GDA office, the receptionist asked me to have a seat and she would let Mr. Christofferson know I was present. Moments later a man entered the room. He stood about 6 feet tall with a slender frame, sporting an olive green velvet hat. His rusty red complexion and handle bar mustache gave him an antique and humorous appearance. When conversing with him, I knew that he was analyzing my every word as if solving a puzzle. His directions were given with authority and an attitude that they had better be followed precisely and faithfully.

There was no nonsense in his approach and his countenance was one that demanded and deserved respect. He was more than a man's man; he was a surveyor's surveyor. His name was John Christofferson but I came to know him as J.C. and I thought that he was J.C. Maybe not in divine appreciation but rather in his magnetic aura that inspired me to be his disciple.

On conclusion of this intense interview, I was employed by J.C. to perform percolation tests sometimes known as perc tests. The purpose was to determine the absorption rate of the soil for a septic drain field. These tests usually took two days to perform. The first day I was to dig post holes 36 inches deep into specified locations, presoak each with water by maintaining the water level to 24 inches from the bottom for at least four hours. The next day I would place water to a depth of twelve inches from the bottom and then every 30 minutes for four hours measure how fast the level dropped. Each time I would make sure it was filled back to the 12 inches mark. I was to affirm whether or not moisture could percolate through this soil area.

It could be quite labor intensive if the soil was hard. It was a deviation from actual surveying, but after all it was measuring the earth and I was out of doors – in nature. J.C. expressed to me that the first rule was to be able to read a map and find the property to be tested. My love for maps and geographical locations paid dividends in that I was able to find each property with relative ease. It served me well with J.C. He liked my sincere approach to the assigned task. I appreciated being treated as a responsible person - a professional. Students need to be taught about what it takes both in learning and the presentation of self, to professional competence.

This first assignment taught me a valuable lesson regarding gates. The person leaves them the way he or she found them; if open leave open, if closed then close it immediately on entrance and exit. On this particular occasion I came upon a closed gate, opened it and for my convenience, left it open. Parking in the middle of the ten acre lot, I hopped out of the jeep just in time to notice two horses escaping through the open entrance. A sense of terror flowed through me as I realized my mistake and the possibility of being fired on my first day. Immediately I sprang back into the jeep and made a bee line to the gate.

Circling to the other side of the grazing horses, I attempted to corral them back to the pasture by waving my arms and yelling. To no avail. In disregard for my responsibility they moved further away to a fresh grazing area which happened to be a neighbor's lawn. Because of the disturbance, it attracted the resident to check out what was going on. Fortunately for me, the neighbor was Richard Wilson, a high school friend of mine that I hadn't seen since graduation.

Quickly delaying the pleasantries, we were able to corral the wayward ponies and coax them back to their place. Relieved that my employment was saved and ever thankful for Richard's knowledge of equine behavior, we caught up on the recent six years of our lives.

One day after a few months of perc tests, I came to work thinking I was going to do another percolation test. Instead, J.C. took me with him to try to recover a section corner. On the way he told me the corner had not been found since it was set in the 1880s. This was an exciting moment for me and I welcomed the change even though I was not sure what it entailed. All I knew was that I was going to go to the field with the legend so I'd better be on my toes. What a great day it turned out to be – a budding surveyor's dream. The learning curve was expanding.

We drove for several miles into the foothills east of Oroville until we came to a dirt road and soon to a closed gate. Ever astute to circumstances of this nature, I knew it was my humble duty to open the gate so I jumped out and obliged. After he drove through, and remembering my previous experience with wandering horses, I closed the gate the way I found it. These gestures would surely be meaningful to my professional future. I had mastered the principles for gate management. I jumped back into the truck. We drove a short distance and pulled over to the side of the road. I sincerely wanted to do what was expected of me as I interpreted J.C., but I was in the dark on our purpose. I was again on the cusp of an 'aha' experience. There was not gate here to open. I kept silent.

J.C. took with him carrying a tall wood staff on which to set a compass, and a measuring tape 66 feet in length. This tape was different from anything I had seen in my nine month's experience with surveyors. Instead of the tape being in Engineer's Feet and decimals thereof, it was divided into links. He explained to me that the federal government measures in chains instead of feet.

Each chain is equivalent to 66 feet and each chain was divided into 100 links making a link approximately eight inches. All that made math sense, but for what purpose here?

Leaving the truck we worked our way through scattered oak trees until entering an open meadow where cattle grazed. With the bovine fans silently observing our movements, J.C. stood on the edge of the meadow and scanned the entire area. After several minutes of not doing anything more and since this was the first time I had worked in the field with him, I felt compelled to ask if I should attend to something. So I asked him if there was anything I should be doing; to which he gave a sideways glance at me and cryptically said, "No." He was in the world of the surveyor's workshop.

Befuddled by the response, I did the only thing I could do - stand there and say nothing. I was watching him but being careful not to make eye contact. To do so would have revealed my abject ignorance. After all he was the Alpha male in this situation. He then began to concentrate on a tiny depression about fifty feet away. Walking over to it, he gave it a closer observation and then instructed me to carefully shave the ground with the shovel going no deeper than one inch at a time. I was at the ready, pleased to be useful. I was still in the dark, but excavating a shovel of dirt an inch on every pass. I could do that, and feel I had some worth.

I correctly assumed that shaving was a horizontal dig achieved by laying the shovel at a slight angle to the ground. I began removing dirt in layers no more than an inch at a time. After a few inches we found pieces of decaying roots. J.C. took a piece of the root, broke it and sniffed it.

He told me that he could tell identity type of trees. It was by the smell and the texture of their roots. I don't recall the type of tree but it was probably an oak - because we were in the foothills of California Mountains – where oaks flourish.

Placing the staff in the middle of the roots, he then connected his compass to the staff. With his eye focused on the compass he turned in the desired direction. Peering over the compass his countenance changed to a look much the same as a cat about to jump on the prey. I was then instructed to hold the zero end of the tape (sometimes referred to as the dumb end – no insult intended) and walk in the pointed direction.

I had only traversed about 30 feet or so when the tape tightened and pulled me to a stop. He told me to go a little to my right and scratch the ground with the end of the tape. I dragged across the top of an 18" diameter rock that was protruding about 6 inches above the surrounding surface. Then with a firmness that left an impression that I had better follow his directions to the T, he firmly said: "Don't move." One wouldn't say he skipped over to me but he was at my side in a moment with an expression of glee and said: "Dig around it so that it is completely exposed, but don't move it."

As I was removing the dirt he placed the staff and compass on the rock. He told me to hold the end of the tape (the dumb end), while he went in another direction of about 50 feet to medium sized brush. He then started cutting the brush with a machete while I made my attempts to uncover the rock. After a few minutes he asked if I was done with the shovel yet. Feeling as if I should have been and which I was not, I replied, "Yes," and took it to him. He then started scraping the ground removing dirt and leaves until he uncovered an old stump about 30 inches in diameter.

There was a sense of excitement in his demeanor but he said nothing. The cows seemed to be wondering, what was the meaning of two grown men scraping the ground. We went back to the rock and he realized that it had not been fully exposed. Looking at me out of the corner of his eye in a manner of disapproval or disappointment found in perfectionists, he merely said, "Dig around it some more."

A few minutes later we uncovered an 18 inches x18 inches x26 inches stone. However, it still had small clumps of dirt on it so we took some water and rinsed the dirt away by using a Wisk broom as archeologists do. As we were cleaning it, he pointed out two sets of grooves which the original surveyor had inscribed in the year 1885. The number of grooves on each set indicated how many sections north and west we were from the southeast corner of the Township Corner.

He then went on to tell me that a Township was six miles by six miles square and consisted of 36 sections. Each section was one mile by one mile. What we had found was the corner to one of those sections. We were, at that moment, the only ones knowing the correct corner of the section made a century earlier. Later I learned that this system was first initiated by Thomas Jefferson.

Much of the order of land division was built on this 'monument' pattern. We had uncovered an old 'monument,' evidence of a legal measurement long hidden, but to be used as legal evidence.

The roots we found in the depression and the stump were the remains of bearing trees. The original surveyor would not only set the stone's for the actual corner but would also set accessories such as the bearing trees to identify the stones location. They would remove a portion of the bark until they found the wood portion then they would usually inscribe "BT" for Bearing Tree and record the bearing (direction) and distance to the stone. This would be done at each corner of the 36 sections and not only the section corners but also at the half mile mark between them called quarter corners. All the while keeping notes of what they did. These notes would then be sent to the Survey General of the United States for approval. Once approved a plat would be prepared and signed by the Survey General or his deputy to be distributed to land offices for sale. When this was done the plats were the order of American soil from sea to sea. The scenario is vital even to national borders. Some South American and Asian nations are at odds with each other over national boundaries because they were careless long ago for setting monuments. The jingle took over: They desperately need either Thomas Jefferson or J.C.

On the way back to the office J.C. addressed the importance of retracing the original surveyor's footsteps. In order to do that one would need to understand and be familiar with the method used to establish those lines. One needed to know some of history's details to keep currency in order to determine land rights. Sometimes that meant measuring in a similar manner the forefathers employed. He pointed out that because of the tools and methods they used they could only obtain limited accuracy. It was not uncommon to find their measurements to be ten to twenty feet different than what we measure today. This can be frustrating as Chief Justice Cooley (1864-1885) wrote in a Michigan State decision:

> "When a man has had training in one of the exact sciences, where every problem within its purview is supposed to be susceptible of accurate solution, he is likely to not be a little impatient when he is told that under some circumstances, he must recognize inaccuracies, and govern his action by facts which lead him away from the results which theoretically he ought to reach. Observation warrants us in saying that this remark may frequently be made of surveyors."

Cooley also wrote in that same decision the duty of the surveyor was to: "search for the original monuments, or for the position they were originally located." A monument being a permanent mark set by a surveyor such as a stake or stone. His reasoning was based on the assumption that "no man loses title to his land merely because the evidence becomes lost or uncertain." His decision set the precedence to the basis of boundary surveys that despite measurements, the original placement of the monument prevails. Otherwise, property lines will be in continual flux. The original line holds. The solution relates to remuneration or some other adjudication, perhaps the courts. Courts have been appealed to for this purpose. During my career I have witnessed the development of sophisticated tools such as GPS, Robotics, and Scanners to acquire precision to within a quarter inch. However, they are only tools that we utilize to locate the agreed positions of property lines and easements. The importance is not necessarily in mathematical precision but in accurate location. From the known beginning we adjust to the shifts that occur in the passage of time. It all makes for a lively business, perhaps seen by the layman in the changes of river beds, even the eruptions of volcanoes. For surveyors it's an accurate line on earth.

Monuments are used to maintain continuity and integrity of neighborhoods, roads, cities, counties, states and countries. Their purpose is to contribute to an orderly society for the placement of infrastructure such as bridges, walls, and utility lines into their prescribed locations. They also assist in flood studies as well as crustal movement of tectonic plates. In South America the conflict over borders of some countries will remain unsettled until neighboring nations will agree on the monuments of borders set many decades ago.

J.C. comprehended all factors of relevance to our world measurements and communicated that to me. He was, for me, a great teacher that day. It worked because I will never forget the feeling of awe and amazement over the fact that anybody was able to scour the country side and find the valuable treasure of identity that was set so many years ago. At that moment I felt the passion and was anxious to learn the skills so that I could acquire the same aptitudes as J.C.; so I became his disciple for my life profession – a mentor that makes a person better in all that he is. There was no going back for me, but to serve mankind in the measurements of earth, vital for a progressive society. God told Adam to "dress the garden and know it." Farmers, ranchers and gardeners 'dress it,' but surveyors know 'it.'

Perhaps my day with J.C. was a test of how well I might work on a field crew. It must have been a passing grade; because when there were no perc tests to be conducted, he would send me with two other fellows on a survey crew. My preference was to be on a field crew where I was able to glean techniques and methods from the other crew members rather than watching water filter away in a hole. Work was steady and helped me support my family but equally important was that I was learning lessons of professional life that were filled with a number of anecdotal messages that were often times laced with humor. When we are of the earth, we are earthy – wholesomely so, I trust.

For example, on one particular day our assignment was to set survey stakes that were to assist a contractor in laying asphalt on an existing dirt road so that it could drain properly. In order to do this they needed us to blue top the finish grade. What this entailed was placing stakes every 50 feet along the centerline as well as both edges of the road. Then we were to drive the stake to where the top would be at a specified elevation. This was done by holding a vertical measuring rod on the ground for the instrument man to read. He would then tell me how high the stake should be above the ground for the finish grade which was usually about six inches. I would then attempt to set it at the proper height and then set the rod on top of the stake while requesting another reading to make sure it was correct. It became quite a contest to see how many stakes I could set at the exact elevation on the first try. However, if the surveyor set it below the grade, he or she lost all points because that meant the stake had to be pulled out, the soil recompacted – so to start over. Once it was positioned properly, we would spray blue paint on top of the stake - thus the term blue top. This was done so the paving contractor would readily know the hubs should be used and those that should not.

The road was located in a part of Butte County where some residents had a less than modest education and influence. Many lived in antiquated mobile homes and camping trailers in desperate need of repair or better yet to disposal and replacement. Some were not livable. The observer would often see improvised additions that consisted mainly of plywood scraps nailed together. It was not uncommon to see outdoor showers and baths surrounded by tarps to give a semblance of privacy. The yards would have a scattering of chickens, while dogs and children roamed freely. Their lifestyle aroused memories of my early childhood and a warm affinity to their situation. When impoverished we tend to make do. These people had even less than we had when I was a lad. These people simply 'made do.' I knew money wasn't everything, but it didn't hurt when everything else was in balance.

One of the locals was driving by in a severely dented pick-up truck with the back window missing and a rag for a gas cap. In the front seat with the driver was a lab mix dog. In the bed of the truck and exposed to the elements was a boy of about 8 years of age. It had all the appearance of a scene out of the movie, "Deliverance." The driver had several teeth missing and sported an assortment of tattoos. The boy was wearing cutoff jeans as his only garment. His face was smudged with dirt. As I recall he had an instrument in hand that appeared to be a banjo.

The driver stopped and asked the usual questions of what we were doing and how long before the road would be completed because: "it gets real muddy when it rains, and when it does, it gets real slick so you can't hardly get out. Lot's o' times we have to pull each other out. It gets to where we have to stay home until it dries up." So it was that scores of vignettes have occurred for me in plying my trade. I am touched by the range of experience in human life – and how people get through – to the end.

In my personal distractions the Party Chief, Dave Goble broke in and said they would be starting construction tomorrow and they would soon have a nice paved road. The local was grateful for the update and put his truck in gear. But before he could leave, curiosity got the best of Dave so he asked "Why is the dog in the front seat and the boy in the back?" The local spit out a stream of tobacco juice and with a nod in the boy's direction said "The boy peed on the rug; least ways that's what the dog says." Then he drove off. It goes to show you that sometimes even man's best friend might sell you out if you're a boy.

On another occasion I was on a job with Dave where we were surveying a property line. Most of the time, distances shown by surveyors are horizontal and not on a slope. The method is to keep the metal tape level and at the same time pull proper tension; all the while steadying the plumb bob over the desired point. (I know the observation suggests work for a contortionist, but it must be accurate.) Usually the rear person, in this case Dave, would hold the metal tape and shout, "Good," when he was steady. At the same time the person ahead, who was represented by me on this occasion, would have the benefit of a leather strap to hold on to while steadying the plumb bob over the point. Sometimes it could take a while to get all components to match up and could be quite a strain on workers' arms. Once completed, Dave would shout figures he was reading in feet and I was to complete it by shouting back what I was reading in decimals of feet. We would then both record our information, his being the field notes and mine in peg notes which was a small one inch by two inches notebook. We could check each other for accuracy, and the construction crews knew they could count on our figures. It amounts to a double measurement. Accuracy is utterly necessary.

While traversing through the back of the lot we came across a three feet tall electric fence that was being used to keep horses from wandering off. We carefully raised the tape over the fence being careful not to touch it lest we receive a jolt. Dave's instructions were crystal clear, that once we established the measurement to not drop the tape because he could get shocked. I forgot the procedure and the shock occurred, which caused a stream of expletives from my partner. My apologies were eventually accepted but for precaution I did not turn my back on him so to offer opportunity to reciprocate. The next day we laughed about it but to this day I keep an eye out for him. These fellows may not believe in revenge, but they often believe in getting even. It is common in baseball that if a hitter is struck by a pitch, a member of his team will likely be accidently hit in the next inning. It keeps everything even – at least in suffering. The umpire may dismiss the second pitcher from the game. The revenge factor is that common and deliberate.

In days of yore and lore; if honor were tread upon then guns or swords would be drawn and a duel would ensue. Even today insults and challenges to one's honor could cause serious repercussions. In professional sports, teams tend to stay clear of insulting another team less it give fuel to the fire of negative motivation. Even in politics, one may refrain from personal defamatory remarks against a group of people because it might be used against them during the campaign. Attitudes of contempt can oftentimes breed discontent and animosity. However, it is sometimes used to incite a person or group to rally their resources to greater heights and more careful performance. Nearly all of my varied experiences have been with colleagues respectful of our profession and working together to 'get it right'; and that with good will for each other.

Teams were generally affirmative to their members, but negative personalities went with the work. GDA had an 'Instrument Man' who tended towards arrogance, and was quite contemptible to those who he felt were beneath him in rank. However, to those above him he would conspire effusive compliment and gratitude. For example he would bring a dozen cookies to work and at lunch offer three or four to the party chief and none to crew members. To him I, and others, were lackeys. He seemed to think of me as the crew pet that would come along on trips and merely there to perform whatever duties that he did not want to manage. I had some ugly reaction thoughts to "get even" with him, but thought better self to avoid 'get even.' We fail when we return negative kind to negative kind. Each person is diminished in some way. Those forgiving of ill will tended to be better workers.

Other times the Party Chief would assign the Instrument Man certain tasks. Because it was not something that he did not care to do, the Instrument Man would then command me to do it. I must say that he was not much of a pleasure to work with and I welcomed opportunities to work on the crew of which he was not a member. These little episodes were learning experiences so to determine if I recognized the dignity and meaning of every human being. It takes some maturation to work well with negative persons, especially when they were in perpetual distemper. One learns to accept others even when they can't be approval of them. I wanted to practice treating others as I wanted to be treated. It took a while to gain satisfaction with that. It is worth the wait, and effort.

On one particular day we were travelling from a job site back to the office. Mike Patterson, the Party Chief, was driving, our friend was in the passenger seat, and of course, I was in the middle. As was usually the case, our comrade began a monologue that was directed to Patterson. Our friend was not paying any attention to the conditions of the road nor did he have his seat belt in place. On the other hand Patterson and I both had our seat belts on when suddenly we came upon a large rut in the road. Our buddy was deep in conversation (mainly with himself) as we crossed a deep cut and did not take notice of the danger nor was he prepared for the jolt we experienced. At that moment for some reason I looked up in his direction only to see his shoulders touch the roof of the truck to which his head had seemingly disappeared into the cavity of his body. It all seemed surreal, similar to what one would see in a Road Runner cartoon. Upon his fallback, the seat catapulted him into the side window and from which he was catapulted back to me. I was firmly strapped in, suffering no negative physical consequences.

After this unwanted display of oscillating action and reaction, he finally settled down. Dazed, he began complaining that his neck hurt. We asked him if he was all right to which he moaned, "Yes." On the way back to the office I too was under a psychological 'evil' from an overwhelming urge to burst into laughter. I agree my reaction was a bit less than compassionate. To put the record straight I have repented repeatedly every time I think of that moment of getting even. I believe in forgiveness - if you don't do it again. Is there really a comeuppance for difficult people?

A few days later, we were working on a construction site with Patterson who was informing me that he planned on taking the state exam for the Land Surveyor in Training (LSIT) in a few months. Passing this exam was one of the eligibility requirements to take the advanced Land Surveyors exam. I asked him, "How much experience do I need to take the exam?"

"You just apply and send in the fees," He responded

Our friend, my nemesis, not one to miss an opportunity to meddle into a conversation said; "Don't bother Ron, you need a lot of experience and it will be waste of your time. I've taken it three times and haven't passed.

If I can't pass, how do you expect to?" (That was a fighting question.) I was determined to pass it.

His words were like a slap across the face as if to challenge me to a duel. My honor was at stake so at that moment I decided that I would accept the challenge. My response was to turn to Mike for a recommendation of a book or two on the subject. After all, if our buddy could not pass the test then why would one want to use his approach? The meddling did work. All things can work together for good if we live an affirmative life in self and faith.

Upon Patterson's recommendations I bought a few books and began my studies. My education was not through a classroom setting but rather it was gleaning information on a day to day basis from JC, Goble and Patterson – and the books. On my first attempt I failed; however, the second was successful. I had completed the first hurdle of becoming a Licensed Land Surveyor. By that time, our friend had moved on so I was not able to gloat to him over my achievement. But I will always be grateful to him for shoving me to greater effort and motivating me to search for excellence. One may not uncover buried treasure with a shovel – sometimes it is done with study, a pen, tools and determination to be what you want to be. Some factors will always be negative, but the affirmative ones far outnumber the negative. The seeking of my place in life was found. My duty from this point forward was to become the best I could be in my life and work. I now had a paper informing the world I was competent to serve on the team.

According to the account in Genesis, Adam was ordered by God "to dress the garden and know it." This meant he would have to learn and understand the land that was entrusted to him. To the degree Adam followed this command; he had to do some surveying thus making him the first surveyor. He did fail at the beginning when he violated the special plot that was monumented for the Creator. He rightly got his 'come-up-ance!' I too had a command and that was to grasp the realization of the talents and inclinations that were gifted to me and the importance of using them for what seemed to me to be a higher call: to know and dress the world garden I live in.

*Visiting grandma and grandpa Asay: Left to Right: Ron, Arnie, Grandma Ella, Grandpa James, Dean, Dad and Mom.*

Putting Big Sticks by Little Sticks

# 10
# Troubling Transitions

*"The laws of nature are but mathematical thoughts of God."*
Euclid

Unsolicited transitions and adjustments are a way of life for all persons. How we respond to those unsought life contexts creates a pattern that we make for ourselves either to succumb as victims or embrace the opportunity to overcome adversity, failure and disappointment. Some wounds are self-inflicted in our choices, reactions, omissions, and private weaknesses. We may paralyze ourselves in our independence and ignorance. We may not include our own depravity in our decisions and actions. Our errors may be less marked in what we do as it is in what we do not do. Believing ourselves mature, we wake up along the way to discover we are short of where we ought to be. If we take self – care and effort with the contexts of our lives we find we can overcome and emerge from the brambles with a sense of balance and victory. It takes some doing and demands energy, faith, change and serious evaluation if we are to evade ultimate loss and failure. Those that choose to overcome are the better for it and find a peace that provides confidence that merges into liberation. It can be a form of steadfastness that bows the neck forward with an intensity that progresses us to victory. The pattern is most clear to me in both my personal and professional life. I am instructed that many people never find the pattern – or don't apply it if they do. Life does not emerge victorious for us if we do not give it some real thought and effort. It is serious business.

In college I took an Advanced Geometry course. The professor's first lecture was of the difference between the geometry we learned in high school and the College Geometry we would now be engaging. High School geometry was basically Euclidian, named after the ancient Mathematician, Euclid, who developed axioms of the basic elements of geometry. We have no clear perception of geometry before Euclid. We students were told at the time to just accept Euclid's ideas as factual. We already knew much of it even if we never had heard of Mr. Euclid. College Geometry, we were told, means proving those axioms and understanding the reasoning behind them and to build creatively on that discovery. We were to move 'higher' in geometry and the understanding of 'things.' The professor carried us along in the story to tell us that Euclidean Geometry is what we may want the world to be while non-Euclidean (College Geometry) is the real world. We see in our applications more than Euclid saw: We want the world to be in perfect shapes of circles, squares, rectangles and triangles. It is a life of innocence – a child's life. The truth is our lives are more like the application of hyperbolics and ellipses with an infinite number of lines intersecting our relationships. These lines can become so entangled that they may fracture under the stress making it difficult to comprehend. We may stall and die. Stop the world, I want to get off. Some persons choose suicide. The applications of life become too much for them. I learned the reality of that lecture suddenly in the collapse of my family world and over time even in my professional world. It was not a progressive loss in my family context, with no preparation for rejection, but sudden – like the sudden crash of a car accident while vacationing on a pleasant journey. What seemed true a moment before was destroyed the moment after. In professional life, it took years of hard work, determination and sacrifice to gain the vision that emerged – about what I wanted to be and what I was willing to do to achieve the goal. The personal seemed to be dying, the professional seemed to be growing and developing.

We open here with my age at 25 years. I had, by this time, found my place in the world. I would be a surveyor and had proven my talent for it. But there was much to do and sacrifices to make to gain a place in the front line professionally in my chosen field.

Personally I had married my sweetheart from high school. We seemed suited to each other in our parental families, in our religious faith, in the birth of our first child, and gradual improvement of our circumstances of life. It seemed perfect for me even though my professional life sent me often far from home. Did that absence have anything to do with the collapse of our marriage? I don't know. Many persons maintain strong marriages in time warps –as in the military.

With a certificate from the State of California that read "Land Surveyor in Training" (LSIT), I felt on top of the world – professionally. At least I had found the work, the occupation, the plan in the context of life where I could do well and serve others in a progressive way. That discovery is vital to the maturity and flow of our lives. It is sought by even handicapped persons in the population. In my context I felt I was on my way. That discovery and euphoria for career and future in my profession was suddenly clouded by events on the home front.

Work was sporadic and income was tight. So much so that we were barely making ends meet with no extras for splurging on items such as new clothes or extravagant dinners on the town. However, I was determined to pursue my calling. I believed that my wife was supportive and patient with what I believed was our mutual vision for my professional goals, and our future financial security as a family. It would take a bit more time. For her there was growing, private impatience with our situation and the lack of a monetary surplus that seems to have contributed to her restlessness. I didn't detect it in the elation of my professional discovery and progress. I must have missed some clues. When I finally detected some, it was too late. I entered a valley of some despair.

The following suggests the events that led upward for my professional life and downward for my family life. It is reflective of the stories of many thousands of marriages and families taken with the contradictions in modern competition between personal and professional contexts of life. Those contexts fight each other threatening failure in one or both personal and occupational success. We were caught in the modern competition of events for our lives – and we were not prepared to manage the tragedy we were falling into. Often times issues become intertwined and are difficult to distinguish so may go beyond repair. Balancing the two seems like a geometric conundrum to which there is no answer for Euclidean minded people like me – or the answer is elusive.

**Personal (or non-Euclidean)**

Surveyors are often depicted as wearing orange vests adorned with a variety of pens and pencils. They may even appear casual wearing straw hats or baseball caps. Plumb bobs dangle for their belts. On established sites, survey flagging and orange safety cones identify their purpose. We tend to be extremely analytical with high proficiency as 'sticklers for the law.' We want our first effort to be accurate. It feels good – saving money and time for all concerned. Prospective clients may be at some odds or differences – either friendly or contentious. Our work demands accuracy and shouts for perfection. It becomes a way of life. On top of all that professional expectation, we are also expected to be people persons. Sometimes that requires sensitivity that is, or seems to be, too extensive to address for peace with contending parties. People differ even about the meaning and application of the rules, the evidence and the outcomes. Surveyors are held to the facts of the world nature – not human nature. This may have more influence on our personal lives than we realize.

Traits of dedicated surveyors lead to viewing the world in formulas to be solved instead of taking the world as it is in the context of sensitive human beings. We discover that some problems are not related to the structures of nature. We are supposed to be above emotions in what we do, but our lives are more than hard evidence. We may have no adequate grasp of emotions in the personal context that means so much to us. It entered in the family of a wife/husband and a little boy to confusion and tragic consequences. This proved true in my relationship with my wife. I had become so self-absorbed in my pursuit thinking that she wanted what I wanted; a career that fit me and would lead to economic security for our future and family. To me it was a simple formula: work hard in a worthy profession needed by society and expect that all else would settle into place. It may not work quite like that vision even for idealistic persons – sometimes impractical, expecting too much. Life is like that – full of expectations if we are willing to sacrifice for them in their formation to reality.

There are other factors at work to form life context including the requirements of persons one is working for, persons who may not factor into assignments in the realities of personal and family life. Nor did I comprehend the complexities involved in faith related to belief in God, even to church activity that called on us for integrity and service. Further, I was so taken with my occupation I had not taken time to mature in my Christian faith so to turn to that resource to solve problems. Our faith and ideals were left to take care of themselves. We had entered the secular atmosphere of American life. We had not paid attention to the life of faith that could have carried us through. That neglected pattern messes up many lives. It must have affected us. We had left our beginning that had brought us together in our parental families. We had become a bit too secular in facing daily life and relationships.

To my surprise and without warning, when I arrived home on a Friday evening to discover that my wife had her personal luggage packed. She told me she was waiting for a friend to pick her up and that she wanted a divorce. No Sunday school class, bible study, or wrestling bouts, or cooking experiences prepared me for the sudden despair I felt at the sight of her driving off with our little Tyler. I stood there alone, in something of a stupor. What happened? The emptiness seemed too much to bear. There was numbness of soul. The whole experience seems beyond language to reproduce.

My parents were living in Porterville, California with my brothers at the time and not wanting to disrupt their lives, I chose not to contact them. However, I needed someone to talk to, so I called my surrogate parents, the Tomlinson's, and they immediately came over to comfort me. They tried to comfort through the evening hours late into the night. They pressed me with words of encouragement. They even confided with recitals of the negative spells they had with each other through earlier years. They assured me that matters would ultimately be alright. After they left, all through the night my sleep was interrupted with questions. Why? What had I done wrong? Weren't promises important? Wasn't marriage supposed to be forever? What about vows and commitments? Was I using the wrong formula? What happened? I thought we were persons of faith – not only in God but in each other. I apparently had taken everything for granted – except for my preoccupation with my occupation. Was it all my fault? I am told that can't be. It may have played a part, but there are other factors to consider. I am told that even if I had done everything right, it might have happened as it did. Life is marked by that kind of mystery. There must be mutual agreement to find fresh start.

In my ruminations, recollections of conversations arose in my mind implying more than friendship between my wife and a mutual friend. Doubts began tumbling in and I presumed that a distracting romance may have occurred. Concerned for my marriage, and with fear of betrayal of trusted friendships; I sat in our modest Dodge Colt and waited in the parking lot where the man worked. On his approach to his grand new Chevy pickup truck I confronted him and asked about my suspicion relative to any intrusion in my marriage and any violation of our friendship. He admitted the truth of my suspicion. Verification only deepened the emptiness and grief that flooded into my being – the double whammy of a broken marriage and violated friendship. Trust had vanished. It had seemed so strong. That too was now shattered. It seemed beyond belief.

My world seemed to collapse around me. My heart sank within me. The realization intensified that the one I trusted the most in life and felt as mine did not feel the same as formerly and further that the context of my related life was also collapsing. It struck me that my wife felt that material accumulation was more important to her than to me. She desired material things that I was unable to provide. It seemed too shallow to me. Overwhelming emotion, almost undefined, permeated my being. It was a sensation similar to hearing a loved one had died only to find they did not share mutual affection and hiding love. We had pledged to each other. Something, I am unable to define died within me. At least it fell asleep and nothing I could do in the months ahead could awaken it.

Monday morning came and my wife had not returned. I went to work anyway thinking it would take my mind off the tragic event for this day. My assignment for the day was to go to the Sacramento area with one of the owners of GDA Engineering, Bill Geddis. On the way I remained emotionally distraught and silent. I attempted to disguise my disheveled countenance by looking out the right door window - away from Bill. To no avail. He asked me if I was alright and I said: "Yes." Sensing that I was not, he reminded me that we had over an hour's drive and that he was willing to listen if I wanted to talk about what it was that appeared so troubling. Gradually, I divulged the reason for my distress and appearance. As the Tomlinson's had done, he reached out to me in genuine concern, a gesture that lifted me somewhat even if his concern could not solve the problem.

He was quiet for a short period and then told me about his recently deceased 18 year old daughter, and his own experience of sorrow related to her. After her birth she was diagnosed with a rare blood disease. Because it was hereditary, he and his wife chose not to have any other children. He proceeded on to tell me of the pain of the loss of their daughter as well as coming to terms with not having any more children. The anguish of realizing their original dreams of having several children and grandchildren would never be realized. Although their circumstances did not generate from a violation of their meaning to each other, their sorrows related to human loss in life changing experience that could not be forgotten and could not be celebrated. Fulfillment in that context would never be realized. The accent was beginning to grip me – that many persons faced life with nearly overcoming denials or disappointments or suffering from which they would either falter and decline, or recover and proceed to fresh contexts. One needs wisdom and great self-effort to avoid collapse and ultimate life failure. There is a future to consider. What would I do to make it worthwhile? Would I surrender to failure or to calamity? I needed prayer, healing and planning for a new life.

To illustrate life's accidental sorrows, Geddis divulged a conversation with a friend about a daughter who was 17 years of age. The friend's daughter became pregnant out of wedlock. His friend expressed that she, in the course of their family culture, had humiliated members of the family. The father was a deacon of the church and he believed she brought disgrace to the ministry. He felt he had to send her to relatives in Utah until after the birth. It was clear that suffering people were trying to find solutions that protected everyone – offenders and offended. The implication was that people can find ways to manage great tragedies and disappointments. Problems are made for solution. Through serious search we find maturity in the process. We gain if we improve ourselves in an awful interim aided by recovery of faith in life and prayer for relief.

Our conversation continued with a bit of surprise. Geddis responded to his friend by saying: "I'll trade my dead daughter for your pregnant daughter." As he told me this, I could see his teary eyes and realized at that point that all my agony and sorrow was shared experience in life and families, and could be even more tragic for them than it was for me. Geddis would prefer his unmarried daughter to be alive and pregnant than to see her in death. I was lifted in the reality of good in an imperfect situation when the participants are sensible and patient. My boy Tyler was healthy and I would be able to see and be with him even if it was only on weekends. I didn't lose my ambition for my professional experience. Even though there was unfaithfulness, I would be able to forgive, so to mend the yawning breach – a breach that had never occurred to be possible for me in life. However, was my wife going to be receptive? The God-given factor of forgiveness, of lifting life and getting on with meaning impressed me. Forgiveness leaped up as the solution to restoration and hope. I felt it worth a try.

With some sleuthing, I was able to gain contact with my wife. Outwardly I expressed my willingness to forgive and wanted to work it out by staying together. At the same time, in the deep interpretation of my soul, the marriage was tainted. Could it ever be as I thought it was? It might not be recoverable. Because the wound was cavernous and excruciating, all I desired was relief. I was a father without my boy. What a sense of loss? I was dazed but hopeful. When would this unbearable invisible load of emptiness be lifted? I felt humbled. With hyperbole in my speech, I emphasized the words of forgiveness to my wife and expressed my contrition by stating it must have been my fault that she set aside our earlier vows for life experience sacred to the meaning of family and the life of love. She seemed to accept my contrition.

We became co-habitants but she was distant about my approach and suggestions. The bloom of our marriage had ended. We pressed on. I felt as if I was bearing the full burden. Stumbling over endearment and believing she would eventually rediscover what appeared to be lost for her. I lived a façade - that all was well or would be. She returned but the declaration of love and fidelity never returned for her. Something seemed wrenched from me that would not return – no matter how hard I tried.

I have learned since that my experience is rather commonplace when the vows of marriage are broken and the love romance has been lost. So strong is the human rapture, according to Scripture that some persons can never get over a break in trust and the growth of love that was lost in the depressing circumstances. No matter what the couple may do, in trying to mend their situation, especially in infidelity, the damage will not be corrected, and life return to the former idyllic context. Recognizing this fact of the human spirit, Scripture permits divorce and remarriage for the offended member. Since divorce is a formidable negative to God, the exception in cases perceived as infidelity permit remarriage – the same privilege afforded to widowed persons. For some persons there is true forgiveness for restoration, perhaps to even better family context following. For some that will never happen, and even they cannot overcome the loss. They must find a way suitable to their natures that permit them to proceed well in life with a sense of fulfillment and joy. It can be done. The evidence suggests that a new context is found for many. For others a stall in the human experience is so stern that there is no restoration. Bitterness and some confusion about human conduct will follow some persons indefinitely. The only solution is true forgiveness for our failures in our affirmations – our violation of fidelity to our vows to each other that affects not only the wife and husband but to the extended family, especially the children – even to society at large.

**Professional (or Euclidean)**

Even though I had an LSIT and thought I would always have a profession, it was the early 80's and the country was in a recession. Some interest rates had touched 15%. Work was sporadic and inconsistent at GDA, so on off days I looked for part-time work elsewhere. Going back to the restaurant business was out of the question. That recourse was not to be used again. I knew what I wanted to do in a profession. So I enlarged my search outside the confines of the Butte County area. With the family breakdown I was facing I was willing to move if needed. Perhaps a move would help recovery of my personal life context to the ideals I had for family life. On May 2, 1983 a previously unknown earth fault uplift triggered a 6.2 earthquake near the town of Coalinga, California. The quake caused an estimated $10 million in damages in the small town. It initiated the geological concept that California was in an even more active seismological situation than had been originally proposed. Studies were launched to determine if there were other unidentified faults. The matter became major for California – and remains so. The situation required the attention of surveyors. That might include me.

The devastation on this occasion was mainly to antiquated infrastructure and buildings. They needed to rebuild and that would require surveyors to verify legal boundaries. My thought was that I could not only pursue my profession but also assist in recovery for the area. I began my shifting life situation by looking for companies in the Coalinga area and found AAK Engineering. My call was transferred to the owner, Ken Valley, who told me he was driving to Oroville that weekend to visit a friend and that he would talk to me then. He gave instructions.

A meeting was arranged at a coffee shop in Oroville where he was having breakfast with his friend. That was all the information I had – no details. Walking in I wasn't quite sure which one of the patrons he might be but was able to deduce it. There was only one table that had two men while the others were populated with families and mixed couples. Valley was middle aged, and medium in stature with a somewhat ruddy complexion and short wavy hair. He had a pleasant demeanor but seemed somewhat casual, even indifferent, in the interview. He accepted my resume but set it aside without even glancing at it. Between bites he asked a few questions but we talked mainly with his friend about life in Oroville. Ten minutes or so after we met I left not sure if it was a productive meeting or not. Life is made somewhat uncomfortable by this common aloofness we seem to show to one another when there is more than two persons in a social event. I was there by his invitation – not an interloper. It seemed like one of those neutral events that occur in our lives – signifying nothing. However, he told me to contact him on the following Monday when he got back to Coalinga. It was a slight encouragement. I presume he simply wanted to see what I looked like on his turf before proceeding. It is a common procedure.

The rest of the weekend I wrestled with the logistics of taking a job in Coalinga and my life in Oroville. I would be leaving family and friends I loved, and an area of beauty for a desert – like area of the Central Valley of California. My wife was indifferent about the proposal to move. She was distant as had become her habit. Even though my marriage was in jeopardy, I was weary and felt I needed to do this for both furthering my career and re-establishing dignity to relieve a prevailing sense of personal depression. Life was becoming a context of toleration. I decided in advance to take the job if offered. There had to be something better for me and for the family – both personally and professionally. Something had to be changed. Perhaps this would be the agent of change to recovery of my first dreams and love. A new environment might be route to family recovery.

On Monday I called Valley. He asked when I could appear there. He went further to offer the use of a small camping trailer parked in the back of his office for my personal accommodations. I was suddenly encouraged. I accepted his proposal and started the following Monday – so to offer sufficient time to wrap up some of my local obligations. One of those was to inform GDA that I was taking the job. When I approached J.C. his response was something that I continue to use when making decisions that are mixed with emotions: "Does it pencil out?" The heart can deceive but facts can draw one back to reality in making good choices. Financially it clearly did "pencil out." Whether or not it would save my family was unknown. I could not 'pencil out' that factor. My schedule would be to work Monday through Friday and I was assured I would have employment for at least six months. The local situation was fluid after the quake. So on Sunday evening I drove the four hours to Coalinga, found the key to the trailer as I had been directed, and felt some anticipation for the week ahead. It seemed like starting over for all of my life. This might be the beginning of a plan to take control of my life. I was going to 'pencil out' better than I had in my younger years – so to 'start over.'

The next morning I was assigned to go with Chris Robles to do a survey in town. Robles was a tall slender fellow with well-groomed dark wavy hair.

He had a professional quality about him but also a sense of humor that made him very approachable. He was an immediate friend – arriving in a time of trouble. His casual acceptance helped me in a new and strange situation. We completed our preliminary work by locating field monuments necessary to establishing the property lines. It was decided since we were in town that we would go back to the office and

I would calculate the position we were assigned to identify. I felt good. It seemed I was already a 'veteran,' and I would prove it in my performance. However, there was more to learn. I 'soaked up' every assignment. I was and am open to learning – even if I dropped out of College as a young man skipping formal education for a family, a family I was now in the process of losing.

Back at the office I was introduced to Tina who was the office manager. Robles started working on another project while I worked on mine. Soon Tina had to run an errand and asked if I would answer the phone and take messages. Of course I would -even though it was my first day on the job and I knew only three new people – Tina, Robles, and Valley.

Not long after she left, a phone call came in asking if Ken Ortina was there. Not knowing who Ken Ortina was or if he worked there or not, I informed Robles that someone was on the line looking for Mr. Ortina. Robles was puzzled and said there was no Ortina who worked here. I then informed our caller that there was no Mr. Ortina here. He responded, "No, I asked if Ken or Tina was there." So began my first foray at a telephone duty – a humorous and modest disaster. I was much better as a surveyor, and that is what I wanted to be.

Soon thereafter, we received another call asking for Greg Featherton. Again I asked Robles if there was a person with that name working here only to receive another puzzled expression. He thought for a few moments then laughed "He's looking for Ken. He is known as the Great Feathered One." Unbeknownst to me Ken was of Native American heritage and many of his clients affectionately referred to him with this name. Apparently my phone skills needed some work, and I needed more information. After a few jovial chidings, I felt like I belonged and quickly made some new friends amongst my fellow workers. Even so, I was pleased when Tina was at her station. This temporary assignment was no better for me than coffee shops. No thanks!

### Personal (non-Euclidean)

However, on the home front I did not feel fresh animation. Arriving on Friday evenings, I would attempt to put on an appearance that all was forgiven and forgotten; but my heart was cautious. Seeking relief from the pain and desiring to start over, I contemplated on the merits of moving the family to Coalinga. It appeared that staying in our home town would not help generate healing. I thought we might start fresh away from the distractions and shame. A new environment might lead to renewed faith and the joys of our personal family. Besides I would have full time work. So the line was drawn by announcing to my wife that I wished to move our family and if she did not agree, I would move from our home. We had to do something dramatic. This was it. She answered simply that she would not move. Our marriage was bankrupt and the only way to possible recovery was separation. I moved, a sad event, but with some relief that a new approach might offer healing. I had to find a way. Life is too magnificent to be lost in despair.

### Professional (Euclidean)

Not wanting to overstay my welcome in the travel trailer, I decided an apartment would serve my lonely needs. Due to the earthquake, housing accommodations were difficult to find in Coalinga so I ended up renting in Hanford. It would be a fifty minute commute but felt it would be worthwhile. The dwelling was simple but modern with a bedroom, bath and kitchen. With the help of my fellow employees, I was able to find ample furnishings. Professionally I truly felt I was on my way. That was a lift for my spirit, but the loss of my family was a prevailing dark cloud that hovered.

Meanwhile with AAK, I was developing my skills by being assigned to the Kettleman Hills hazardous waste disposal site, a major project in California. It is located in rolling hills about thirty miles southeast of Coalinga near the roadside oasis of Kettleman City – on Interstate Highway 5. Because it was a dumping site, it had peculiar odors that weren't the same aromas I experienced while working in the restaurant business. And the desert scenery was far different from the back drop witnessed while working for the Forest Service in northern California. The important thing was I was gaining professional knowledge and taking on the duties of a party chief. One of my jobs was to stake ponds for liquid waste. These ponds were constructed so that the discarded fluid did not permeate the soil and seep eventually into the water table. Significant precautions were taken to assure proper depth of the layers of clay and liners were correctly placed. Eventually the fluid would evaporate leaving the chemicals behind in the sludge. This sludge would then be carefully excavated and placed in pits as solid waste. The kind of project is vital to the modern style of life that manages great quantities of waste material. To do it safely is a difficult problem. The general public has little idea about the effort and cost of the treatment of waste – a treatment that affords a gargantuan service for the personal convenience of our citizenry. It has created an expensive industry.

For solid waste, authorities must keep extensive records of not only what was being placed but also where it was located before they buried it. My other duty with my crew was to place stakes in a hundred foot grid pattern with not only the horizontal coordinates but the vertical location as well. They would then log the location of the item from those stakes. It was a necessary work requiring a surveyor's skills. It was great for me.

Sometimes the solid waste would be very interesting. For example, rumor was that they placed a fifty gallon barrel of cocaine from a drug bust. It sounds attractive to addicts. However, the material was laced with diesel and other chemicals – making it impossible to use for any person. Another time, I saw a truck dumping what appeared from a distance to be a green glob of goo. I discovered it was actually money that had been shredded. The site managed with reasonable security with safety for the future generations in mind. The project was well designed and managed.

**Personal (non-Euclidean)**

I was becoming accustomed to my new way of life when my wife contacted me saying she wanted to work things out. She was willing to move and start over. It was also during this time that Coalinga was suffering from aftershocks and caused great anxiety for Valley's wife. So much so that they decided to open a satellite office in Bakersfield. Because he had not yet established a stable clientele in that area, I would divide my time between Coalinga and Bakersfield. This caused uncertainty about where we were going to establish residency. To add to it, we received the wonderful news that my wife was pregnant with our second son, Aaron. This may have given rise to the mutual proposal that we try sincere reconciliation. Taking this all into consideration, we decided to stay put in Oroville until after Aaron's birth and AAK was more firmly established in Bakersfield. There was some lift that personal solutions might be found. There was movement and it seemed like it was in the right direction. There was a ray of hope. I felt some lift.

Aaron arrived in July 1984 and again I was the most proud of fathers. Celebration was interrupted due to our move to Bakersfield. We temporarily set up residence in a townhouse and soon thereafter bought a new home on the south side of Bakersfield. We began establishing roots by becoming acquainted with our neighbors and a church. The Church had meant so much to us in our romantic years. Perhaps we could find our way again – with new friends sharing values that offer peace, love and balanced lives. I was poised to give it a fresh try, even if it was not recovery of the earlier romance and warmth. I wanted to get on with family life.

### Professional (Euclidean)

Life was on an upswing and it felt good. I was working directly under Valley's direction and he taught me more about the tools and accidents of the trade which were sometimes a bit unorthodox. For example, one day we were looking for a survey monument in an oil field. Records indicated it was 4" diameter brass cap set on a 2" iron pipe. We needed to find the brass cap. Otherwise we would end up having to look for other control evidence in the area thus increasing the costs of the project. Both of us went to the proximity of the place we thought the specific monument would be found. With four eyes of two men thumping the ground, we might find it.

We took the pipe locator which makes a screeching noise when placed over ferrous material. Listening for a sound we discovered that the ground was what surveyors call "hot" - meaning that the area held an excess of metal so to make it difficult to identify a specific spot. This meant that we were going to have to be extremely fortunate to locate this monument. The mystery plot thickened.

We then began to look for any indications of where the monument might be such as a guard post, wood lathe, flagging, or indentations in the ground. Ken soon began scuffing at the ground with his foot and uncovered the top of the brass cap for which we were looking. However, it was lying at a 45° angle to the ground with about 3 inches of the pipe still intact and attached. Apparently it had been severed by a grader and clearly out of position. We knew only that we were near the actual place of the monument.

Picking up the cap he looked at it and said: "They say if you spill some salt, throw some over your shoulder for luck." He then threw it over his shoulder behind him to which when it hit the ground we heard a clank sounding like the hitting of metal on metal. We looked at each other and said at the same time: "No way!" Immediately we went to the place where the brass cap made impact and discovered the rest of the pipe. When testing to see if the severed portion of the brass cap coordinated with the pipe in the ground, it fit perfectly. "Impressive. I have never seen that method before. I'll have to remember it," I said. He just smiled back as if to say: "nothing to it." Sometimes it is better to be lucky than smart. Sometimes it is dubbed as creativity. But sometimes there isn't anything else to do. Perhaps angels do help us in what we call 'chance.'

**Professional and Personal (or Geometry)**

My time with Valley and AAK was filled with mixed blessings but most of all it was a time to mature, to find my way, and come to terms with the complexities of life and relationships, even though I do not agree with some of society's ways and feel uncomfortable with much of it. No one agrees with all matters especially dynamic life and society. The secret is found in maturity – a meaningful way of life by faulty persons dealing with faulty people in a faulty society. When we mature we can manage so much better than in our younger years. We are called to maturity.

A few years later, my wife and I did divorce not able to overcome the problems that seemed to have no solutions – at least none we could discover to family unity. We groped for answers but they never really came. Maybe we just outgrew youth and traversed different paths. Perhaps she was impatient yearning for security while I searched for my own career path. Then again maybe she may have been a realist while I was an idealist. Whatever it was we didn't deal satisfactorily with the fault lines of our lives. Some might say: "What a shame." It is a shame that decent persons do not find solutions to some matters. However, pity is not the answer but rather the response. We should be making the choices to surmount the obstacles and seek victory by continually balancing Euclidean pragmatism (application of the system) with non-Euclidean romanticism (the system itself). It is both human and divine. Adequately searched, found and applied it offers much of idealism. It is more likely found by penciling it out, than tossing caps over our shoulders and hoping that accidents or chance will give us answers.

*Tyler and I backpacking over Kearsarge Pass*
*in the Sierra Nevada Mountains.*

Putting Big Sticks by Little Sticks

*11*

# *Life's Varied Concepts*

*"Which foot do you want?"*
*Mark Gilbert*

There are many reasons advanced for leaving a place of employment. A large number of workers leave jobs or are terminated every year. They are positive and/or negative – depending on the context of each life. They vary from need for greater income and/or benefits, a change in career goals, a search for a more fitting life work, and the like including boredom. (Think 'fry cook'!) Of course workers may just get fired – and that for various reasons. I resigned three times from the same employer – from sheer boredom. I feel like I may have experienced many of the causes at one time or other along the way. My work at AAK was steady, and the wage adequate. However, soon after our move to Bakersfield in late 1985, I began feeling as if the assignments we were properly carrying were more technical than professionally analytical. It all was important to clients but was becoming somewhat boring for my searching mind and attitude. Whatever the reason, I wanted more, and that not tied to income. Our work seemed more to do with calculations for common problems than investigation and research. I preferred the latter – when I could get it. There were challenging moments that whetted my appetite – even when I was a fry–cook. (Remember the liver and onions recipe.) There developed a growing yearning to understand deeper theory and practice than I had been given and greater challenge in the applications of Land Surveying technologies. Mathematics, although fitting to my reported skills, began to be mundane and robotic while the inquiry into various practices and mysteries brimmed with promising excitement for me.

Some of my old chef-feelings of boredom crept in. I began feeling as if I was being 'pigeon- holed' into a methodical repetition of grinding out positions of pond locations. Inside, I began yearning to understand boundary resolutions and the inner workings of project development. I did not warm to repetition. (I am told that it is common complaint that sometime leads to inferior work done.) Some of my friends turned on it – with satisfaction. I yearned for greater challenge and participation. I have also been informed this expansive spirit is a good sign related to creativity. It is seen as a motivator to move on in the artistry of work and discovery. The attitude has much to do with creative life and fulfillment.

Seeking a change in venue, I applied for a position at the eminent Martin-McIntosh company. I gained an interview with Roger McIntosh. He was a civil engineer and had an easy demeanor about him. Clean cut, he seemed to reflect the typical yuppie appearance prevalent at the time. We interviewed well. I was impressed with his professionalism. The environment seemed greatly elevated in professional context than I had experienced earlier in any employment. There was less casualness, greater refinement. His office was well organized and everything seemed to have its place. Here was serious business and challenging projects. My thoughts were that I very much wanted to work for him and this company. It would help me in my vision and movement forward perhaps upward. He asked me when I could start. I told him I would need to give two weeks- notice to my present employer, AAK. He was in agreement and thought it admirable in respecting my duty. It was clear that he would expect the same response from me if I were to move on from his corporation. The experience was pleasant, and gave the proper and growing professional 'feeling' I always hoped to acquire. Here was an opportunity. The casualness of my early experiences was yielding to more professional patterns. Further, the salary would improve and responsibility would increase. My dreams seemed about to become reality – professionally. (None of this new motivation was seen as put down of previous opportunities. I was moving along as I gained knowledge and application. I am grateful.)

I gave my resignation notice to Mr. Valley. He took it in stride and did not demonstrate any feelings that I should go or stay. I believe he understood my growing professional dream. The experience had rounded out my education in the basics of the business. I wanted to gain status in the profession I loved. I felt that somewhere there was greater fulfillment for me.

I arrived on Monday morning at Martin McIntosh as agreed and was instructed to report to Gene Martin, the partner of the firm. Martin was a professional Land Surveyor and in charge of crew assignments. With a light complexion and a medium build, he also seemed to have a kind of fierceness about him. His first greeting was not "How are you?" Or: "Glad to have you aboard." He stated: "I wish I had a say in hiring you." I was unsure what that meant at this point. He might say it to his partner. I was new to his team. I felt unsure of his approach which was not that unusual in the give and take of authority people in some business contexts. It couldn't be a good sign, and is an inferior approach to professional life. Was I being put down? His attention wasn't easy-on 'the new kid on the block.' He led me into his office where he shuffled through desk papers - perhaps to find some information to give to me. While waiting, I noticed a plaque on the cadenza that read: "Diplomacy, the art of being able to tell someone to go to hell and they look forward to the trip." Maybe that is what he was implying, but I wasn't sure I would look forward to the trip. Was this to fulfill my dream? We are rightly appalled at such an approach of persons to persons in life transitions. But, we worked out a schedule. I continue to wonder why a good partner would take away from a new person the good his partner had engendered.

He paired me with Felix Esquivel. Esquivel had a rather large physical build, but not overweight. His Latino appearance and serious nature caused me to be a bit intimidated. I soon found out that my concern was warranted. As we traveled through the farm land of southern Kern County he informed me that he was a Vietnam Army veteran and had been assigned the unenviable tasks as a marksman. At the time he did not go into details about his duties but I could tell they haunted him. They carried over to his rapport with others. It is common for us to permit our negative experiences to dilute our respect for others. There has been wide distribution of stories of servicemen needing considerable aid to recover from the experiences of bloody confrontation. My colleague had such a story. Violence and bloodshed make different persons of those fed on a diet of such negatives in life to death. Our lives are best when built on affirmations. God is affirmative to us.

Soon we arrived at our destination which was 160 acres of fallow farm land to be planted into an orchard. Our job was to set up a grid pattern so that they could place both the trees and the irrigation system in the correct locations. So it was that we began work together. It was a worthwhile project, and would contribute to my hope to become a fully equipped person in my field of dreams? Feeling duty to my daily assignments I pressed forward – with some trepidation.

While setting up the equipment to begin our measurements, I noticed that the area was completely calm with no breeze or noise. Accustomed to the city with traffic noise and the occasional horn honking or maybe a siren, I was warmed by the serenity. That aroused my own pleasant memories in the woods with my dog, and in the first day of my work as surveyor in mapping the forest road. Expressing my pleasure to be in such a peaceful location; Esquivel responded with a cackle: "Yeah, so quiet that nobody can hear the screams when someone kills you." Suddenly the serenity was diluted from my earlier days in the woods. The beauty, silence, peace were smeared a bit. The beautiful earth seemed stained with life in distortion with life-changing warfare. So much of my idealism seemed to be always challenged in the context of my sensitivities. You can only imagine the degree of terror that overwhelmed me – which seemed like a shuddering of soul. Observing my discomfort, he laughed and said: "Just kidding." That off-handed remark did not carry much solace for my nature. In attempt to avoid upsetting him I made sure I did what he asked me to do without argument or debate. I would get through the day. Perhaps he was using some sort of reverse psychology to improve production or maybe he was reverting back to his days in Vietnam. I went through neutral motions for the rest of the day. Sociologists find that many persons live their lives in that context – just get through the days. Both of us were men in need, but neither perceptive enough to help the other.

In an attempt to put me at some ease, he gave me a brief history lesson of the wind storm that over took Bakersfield in 1977. He could tell a story in detail. The storm lasted several days with dust roiling one mile high and traveling 90 miles north to Fresno where it literally rained mud. He pointed to the nearby two inch square wood fence posts and informed me they used to be six inches square. He recited how the abrasive dust literally removed the hide from cattle. In Bakersfield, swamp coolers tore from their placements and soared to heights and distances until dropping several blocks away. I was being educated on the negative powers of nature – a nature so pleasant to my thoughts and feelings. What is magnificent to one person may be threatening to another. In any event, by the end of the day I began to understand his sense of humor, his life influenced by tragedy and terror - but more importantly his strategic approach to the work at hand. I had learned something more about human nature and the profession I so highly valued for my life. In retrospect the day served me about life and meaning. What began as a tumbling experience in human context became useful to my life not only in professional competence, but to build respect for persons quite different from my preferred orientation. It was a good day. Some bad days turn out to be good days. (We need to know that, and remember it when we need it.)

During those days Martin McIntosh operated with two survey crews. One of the Party Chiefs was Esquivel and the other was Mark Gilbert. Oftentimes I was shuffled between Esquivel and Gilbert depending upon the type of work to be performed. My skills were elevated. I was interested and learning new patterns doing what I loved and lived professionally to do – in nature's surroundings.

On one occasion, Gilbert and I were assigned to layout a rather large building. Its function, when completed, was to be used for a Medical Center. Buildings have columns that are strategically placed so must support the beams that span from column to column. Our job was to provide stakes in a pattern so that when string lines were attached to our hubs they would cross at the center of each column. It was imperative our tolerance be within 1/8 of an inch. In order to meet the criteria, we made sure we had the proper equipment to meet this close standard and the essential tools to carry through procedures. One of those tools was a calibrated steel invar tape. This measuring tape has an extremely low expansion and contraction rate when exposed to temperature changes. A tape the length of one hundred feet will expand or contract about 1/8 inch for temperature changes of fifteen degrees from the standard of 68 degrees Fahrenheit. In addition the tape has a low stretch factor when under stress. (Now you know how to set large foundations. Easy sounding but not so easy to do. The lay reader may already feel lost for this event. Stay with the story anyway as our point will become clear in a kind of developing confusion.)

We completed the assignment by early afternoon and went back to the office. Gilbert decided to go home. I stayed at the office to become more familiar with the company's computer programs. Shortly after Gilbert left, the secretary approached me and asked: "Did you stake that building this morning?" I affirmed that we did. She informed me that the contractor called saying it was urgent he talk with either Gilbert or me. Something serious to the project was 'wrong.'

I called the phone number. The contractor answered and sounded desperate: "Ron, we have a problem out here. Nothing is fitting. We are missing you guys anywhere from 1 to 4 inches. Is there any way we can get you to come out today and check it. We scheduled concrete trucks in the morning at 6 and I would hate to cancel. They might not get back for several days. If that happens it is going to throw us off schedule." I knew that would be costly and troublesome. His call was appropriate to the problem.

Contacting Gilbert at his home, I informed him of the situation. He told me he would be there in 30 minutes. I too headed for the site. When we arrived, the contractor was quick to point out that the distance between our stakes was supposed to be one hundred feet. Instead he was measuring 100 feet 3 inches in one location and 99 feet 10 inches on another. He went on to inform us that everywhere he measured, the distances were not consistent.

With the superintendent in tow we went to each stake and measured exactly 100.00 from our steel invar tape. The contractor was befuddled and replied: "I don't understand, we measured it and we got different distances." Gilbert then asked him to get the tape that he had used for the purpose. The contractor disappeared into the job trailer and came out with a fiberglass tape. The problem was the rigid tape in conflict with the more dynamic measuring tape. (Such differences are rather common consequent to the development of new tools for about everything.) His tape was not a tape that included the needed margin for earth dimensions and dynamics. Interest and excitement were rising, as was our relief for having done the work as it needed to be done. We wouldn't have to change a thing – not an inch.

Gilbert and I looked at each other and then back at the contractor. Gilbert then asked for the tape from the contractor and instructed me to go to one of the stakes and he would go to another. He then told me: "Hold on to the tape as tight as you can, no matter how hard I pull." As I strained to hold on, Gilbert first pulled the tape over the point to where it read 100 feet and then he pulled even harder so that the 99 foot mark was over the stake. He continued to pull in an attempt to obtain the 98 foot mark. As he did, the stressed tape narrowed from ¾ inches to ¼ inch wide.

Under strained breath Gilbert asked the contractor: "Which foot do you want?" We could give him whatever he wanted – accurately. There was a touch of humor in the question. Gilbert knew we were correct in the measurements and so did the contractor. Our measurements allowed for nature's 'movement' so to withstand storm. In an event of great storm, with his measure the columns might collapse.

Without saying a word the contractor gathered the stretched tape to his chest, walked over to the dumpster, threw it in, and asked us where he could get a steel invar tape. The alleged problem was solved and we went back to the office with a humorous story to tell, and store for the future. There was some satisfaction in the telling. The contractor should have known what he learned that day. Modern professionals must be continuing students of their trades. Not all have been to the embarrassment of the true professionals.

Shortly after this incident and trained to take on sophisticated assignments, I was informed that I was going to be contracted to Chevron to plot the location of oil wells on their maps. That meant that I was going to report to the Chevron office each work day for the next six months. Here was a new challenge, and new people. I met Tim Mack. Mack was medium in stature and sported a bushy mustache that spooned over his upper lip. His manner was receptive as he began showing the well plats and the large maps to which the wells needed to be plotted. He went on to tell me that I would need to review over 1,700 wells that Chevron owned in the San Joaquin Valley and make sure they were plotted correctly on master plats. These plats were used by geologists and engineers to design future locations and replacements of spent oil wells.

This was all 'big stuff.' Even though this was a major project for a new guy at Chevron, I was gaining new friends and advancing my skills. We 'weren't' always working so became personal friends as well as colleagues. We seemed always to be thinking of some 'fun.' When well occupied humor seems like a must to our lives even when we are serious and engaged. Fun contributes to balance. It belongs even in our sacred moments – on occasion. One morning Tim and I were sitting in the survey office with the door open, and casually discussing the plans for the day when a beautiful young woman walked by our door and down the hall. We sprung to our feet went to the door and peeked around the corner watching - as she disappeared into an office two doors down the hall. Who was this attractive female visiting the realm of men? Just as she disappeared, we regained our professional senses. Tim's supervisor was standing at the doorway and asked: "Do you want to meet her? She is an intern from the college and will be here for the summer working with drilling and production." We jumped at the opportunity and followed him to the office but just as we were entering, I leaned over and whispered in Mack's ear, "You have a booger in your mustache." He was startled, but couldn't escape the office situation.

Mack's immediate response was a look of horror as he placed his hand over his mouth and nose. He began rubbing in a muffled attempt to remove the announced obtrusive booger. Of course there was no such issue of embarrassment to mar his fine mustache but I must say he could not take his hand from his nose and mouth region for fear that there may possibly be an offensive physical factor related to his appearance. So during the whole introduction Tim was extremely uncomfortable and it showed, while the rest of us displayed a suave approach in greeting our new colleague. The offices seemed to have immediately become more attractive with our new intern. The addition raised the cultural level of general male casualness. There may have been a miracle of improved male conversation and refinement that emerged. As we walked out of the room, I had a big grin on my face, Mack announced, "There was no booger was there?" He then shook his head and smiled as if to say 'good one, I'll get even.' (He did.)

We were always showing our creativity in our practical jokes with each other. (Such is the life of men who work together, like each other, but beating' gotcha' jokes with each other from time to time with what are called 'practical jokes.' Practical? They don't work well with some persons who find it difficult to bond with others in that context. (It appears commonly with athletes.)

I had forgotten all about the booger incident when 10 years or so later Mack and I met to catch up on the years. His first comment as we greeted was: "You've got a booger on your mustache." As a joke, I didn't fall for it at the moment but shortly excused myself and made exit to the men's room to check in the mirror - just in case. One can never be too careful. Some of our fun was life changing – at least as it relates to mustaches. The score is tied one to one. The tom-foolery will remain with us for our lifetimes.

It took me about four months instead of six to complete the plotting. However, Mack was impressed with the work and reporting – coming in earlier than expected. This was the deeper stuff I had looked for. He wanted to keep me on with Chevron to help assist in staking well locations. There was time remaining on my contract with his office. I was teamed up with Mark Godfrey who really did not have any survey experience but Mack wanted me to teach him how to operate the equipment. The student was now to become a teacher.

Godfrey was a sports enthusiast, particularly baseball with high loyalty to the Los Angeles Dodgers. I, of course, am an avid San Francisco Giants fan – hailing from northern California. The truth is I have two teams I root for; the Giants and whoever is playing the Dodgers on any day. Oftentimes at home while watching a Giant-Dodger game, the Dodgers would score a run and the phone would ring just once. Immediately, I knew it was Godfrey gloating so I would reciprocate by doing the same when the Giants scored. It is all in great fun – from boogers to baseball. I wonder if life can be bonded with others if they are unalike to find the 'fun' moments – even in some serious matters. All of this is a part of the residue of the child in the man for some of us. The casual personal exchanges season our lives for good – if meant for good and not dangerous. It depends on the style a person prefers to follow. The casualness and trickery works for some – not for all. The point is to develop some silly distraction that keeps us from taking self too seriously. It is a part of human bonding – a special gift to our lives. It seems particularly suited for the male gender. For us it seems to beat knitting blankets together – although some he-men have done that.

During this Chevron episode of months, Godfrey coached and organized a men's softball team that consisted mainly of Chevron employees. The reader already surmises my interest – baseball at any level win or lose, suits me just fine. The name chosen for the team was the "Vigilantes." However, due to a misprint from the printer the shirts read "Vigilants." The tailor must never have heard any Spanish. The shirts were not returned. We were vigilant. The team was very active and would play almost every weekend at a tournament. In fact we played over one hundred games that year which caused me to spend a lot of time away from home. This may have contributed to the strain on the home front, a divide that had never healed fully from the earlier break. In my new-found professional life my personal life at home was losing its way. Neither my wife nor I were working hard enough to save our marriage. In the enthusiasm for work and play I must have missed something that may have sundered my family. For the purpose neither of us appeared vigilant.

Soon my term was up at Chevron and I went back to reporting at the Martin-McIntosh office where I was back with Esquivel. Our new assignment was to set grid points along the right of way of a railroad in Coalinga. There was a serious spillage. Apparently, this track supported railcars that had carried asbestos. The dangers of asbestos for the respiratory system were known for some time but it wasn't until the 1980s that the material was banned in use for construction. The matter became serious for all communities. At the time of this writing it remains so.

We had to go through extensive safety training on identifying asbestos as well as the proper use of protective clothing. We were first required to go through a station that distributed protective apparel that covered the entire body except the face. The face was guarded with a mask that filtered outside air. We wore these suits along with the other workers who were doing the actual clean up. Despite our "moon suit" appearance, the local residents went about their business as if nothing was unusual. The people of Coalinga are known to be quite friendly. In fact they would often come up to us and greet us. They seemed unafraid, while knowing we were fully protected. We often found the public casual about human dangers – even though well informed of that danger. This casualness is sometimes a major factor in solving society's problems. On one occasion a resident at the local A&W Root Beer stand, greeted us while standing a few feet away as he nibbled on his fries. He was unprotected. I was taken aback - knowing the dangers of this material and its ability to permeate human tissue when spores might be circulating in the air we are breathing. Many persons have not adjusted to the many dangers of modern life. Our freedom gets the best of our conduct in a dangerous world. It is seen most fully in the way we drive our cars and trucks. We seem to have limited information about the context of our lives.

During these months, so taken with my professional life, the home front continued in decline. My wife accepted a job working as receptionist for a local surgeon. Our relationship was further strained, perhaps as already noted due to my work out of town and the weekend softball excursions. Over the years I have come to the realization that I enjoy being active, both professionally and off the job - to the detriment of my domestic home life, which is by nature more sedate. Even so, the evasion of one or both of the members of a marriage to serious discussion, and the differences in life interests may create an impossible situation for the couple and the children. Melody responded to her own distractions, unacceptable to our original vows. Analysts would likely find we were on separate wave lengths as we grew older and both persons looked for more from life than they were receiving. The fires of youth and romance had abated. We had lost what we believed in the beginning to be the eternal for us. It is a major matter for many marriages. We can only blame ourselves, but blame doesn't solve problems.

It was early May, 1987 when I picked up Tyler and Aaron from the baby sitter after work around 3pm. Tyler was excited that he was going to have a birthday party at our house and wanted to hand deliver his invitation to a friend. I agreed that he could ride his bike to his friend's house a couple of blocks away. In his exuberance to get there he was not checking traffic and hurriedly entered the street. He was hit by a car. One of his friends rushed to the house to inform me of the situation. Quickly gathering up Aaron, I hurried to the scene where he was lying face down. His right arm and leg were in awkward positions. Horror filled me. I caught my breath. The emergency responders carefully lifted him on a gurney to the ambulance and transported him to the hospital. Arriving at the hospital with Aaron in tow, I attempted to contact my wife at work but had to leave a message with an answering service which I thought odd since she would be answering the office phone at that hour. Surely she would want to know about the accident and I would help her through this tragic event. I couldn't find her.

Soon Tyler was evaluated by the doctor, and was making good recovery. There was concern that a couple of spinal discs may have been displaced. However, upon closer evaluation the examiners determined that the issues related primarily to a congenital problem with no need for present alarm. The relief was dramatic aside from a few scrapes and bruises, he was released a few hours later but I was told to monitor his condition throughout the night. There was rejoicing, but something was missing. Mother wasn't there on time to enjoy the good news – with thankfulness. Something was absent, never to return again. This was the real beginning of the end of our once beautiful family.

During the whole ordeal of time I was calling the house to let my wife know where we were and what happened - but no answer. It wasn't until around 7pm that she came to the emergency room and within 10 minutes the surgeon, to whom she was employed, entered the hospital. The whole incident seemed surreal and it suggested that something was radically amiss in my inability to contact her.

Our natural concern about our boy covered the problem for the days of Tyler's recovery. In fact it wasn't until a few months later while on a back packing trip with Tyler that I had a premonition of my wife leaving our family for the Doctor and there was nothing I would be able to do about it. Once again the realization of broken vows, perhaps for material gain, crept into my thoughts and our family life. Granted, self-absorption in recreation and career may have caused me to distance myself during some periods, but it was not enough to rationalize infidelity and the fracture of family, affecting the lives of our two sons. Justification for such behavior may seem logical and appropriate to the offender but in reality it equates to departed values and slothfulness. She seemed to value material wealth more than I did. The hard work of a true relationship takes mature wisdom we did not find. Trust issues needed healing that could only come from her to me. She was not inclined to seek healing in life identity with another person, and I lost any hope for my/our marriage. It had survived one earlier break in our fidelity. It could not survive two.

Even so, there also seemed to be a divine embrace that reassured me that I would not endure this personal tragedy alone. Perhaps the rise of courage was caused by previous encounters that permitted a growth in maturity or maybe it was because I was beginning to accept a faith that would cover things I did not understand. My faith carried me through – for both me and my boys. My family sorrows became motivations for me to find maturity and incorporate a spiritual discipline to my life. It gave direction to human relationships in all areas of daily experience. I became more determined than I had ever been. I determined not give up. I would survive, and so would my boys. Life was given to be fulfilled – so victorious. It would take fresh dedication. There would be a fulfilling future, if I would give attention to it.

Arriving home in July from the backpacking trip, I wanted to share Tyler and my experiences in the wilderness; but instead, my wife informed me that she found an apartment and was moving out. This time I could only return a forlorn smile, paused, and responded: "O.K." I then proceeded to unpack my gear. No scene was created of crying or begging. My hopes had trickled away after Tyler's accident. They had been challenged earlier, and I had recovery hopes now lost. I had been properly prepared this time and accepted it. She packed what she wanted to take and left with our sons - our boys.

After her departure, some peace and confidence comforted me as I felt a new life chapter was about to begin. I seemed to have been prepared for this tragic moment. It seemed surreal. The marriage had become so bland that the break seemed like a release. Actually, it was a sense of relief with no feelings to contact family or friends for counsel. My directions were clear that there would be continuance in life and that I had nothing to fear for meaning and the future. I would project my life, and find victory in it. There is a refuge in the storm. There was something spiritual in the change. I would find a way – and a way with my boys.

A few weeks later I was served papers at work, creating some renewed personal disillusionment. I had asked her not to send them to my office but that request was disregarded, I did not want to suffer that embarrassment. Even that unfeeling gesture I soon accepted. I wanted a spiritual lift, and no ill will even in the loss of my family – stated in the strong appeal of romantic love some years earlier. We were unprepared for so early a marriage. Adult interests in variances caught up with us.

To cover my loss I began to give even more time to my profession. Computer aided drafting programs were beginning to take root and were more affordable for Engineers and Architects. During this time I took a beginning AutoCAD class at Bakersfield College. I sought to become the best I could be in my profession – a fulfilling context that, like my faith, contributed to carry me through the pain of my departed family. With Winston Churchill facing unbelievable odds: never! Never! NEVER! Give up.

McIntosh learned that I had taken a class and brought me in from the field. He wanted me to work on drafting the Asbestos cleanup in Coalinga. Wanting to be a truthful team player, I agreed, despite telling him that I was not yet on the same level as the specialist in the details of that field. Mapping programs required more than fulfilling those plans in the field. The field had become my preference – not the inside planning only. This acknowledgement may have eventually led to my demise at the firm. I was determined to press on, no matter the barriers and my advancing years. I did want to be genuine.

I was advancing well but not yet prepared to produce at so high a level. With high expectations, I endeavored to meet the challenge. Even though I worked after hours to make up for my inexperience in this arena, I could not make up the lost time. It is often an uneasy transition from field to office. Maybe it is due to the ever changing scenery of field situations with its creativity, daily repetitions versus the office setting that doesn't suit this or that person. Loving nature as I do, the details of office work did not seem as attractive as some persons find it. I love outdoors action, and that part of the problem-solving business of the surveyor. With a sense of family loss, I pressed on feeling some tension hanging over me, I pressed on feeling further personal loss in the extensive new professional assignment.

After a few months I was released with the explanation that I did not meet the essential requirements of being a CAD drafter. It was my own initial protest – not accepted at the time, but now announced to me as something just discovered.

With the end of my appointment and the impending divorce, I was devastated. I was in another 'downer.' Is life to be measured by a series of up and down experiences? Couldn't anything be 'nailed down?' Once again I had to lean on prayer to understand and bear what was turning out to be a life tangle in a complicated world – sometimes harsh. I was old enough to have a better context. Lessons are distributed throughout our lives to cause deep reflection into meaning and character. Oftentimes we do not want to deal with life factors and choose to blame others rather than coming to terms with our own flaws, perhaps omissions. If we are honest and seek truth, harm will not likely follow.

Cleansing can take place as we kneel in vulnerability and humility to God who made us, and gave us directions about mother earth, family, and service to self and mankind. Somehow I held on to that when my values were being challenged. The process carried me through the ordeal.

Life is filled with opportunities to transition from a repetitive technician to a practicing professional. The measuring tape of our lives is available but self-esteem may war against it for survival. A battle ensues between the mundane formulas of life and risky theoretical applications. Those that align properly with both the principles and practices will find victory for life that passes understanding. Eventually we accept providence and embrace life on a higher level than mere humanism. Only then can vision be formulated that originates from the creations' creator. We may feel like giving up. There is reason to shout inwardly to 'NEVER GIVE UP! ' With patience, seeking that includes orientation of mind and spirit, with faith and prayer, and in faith with that prayer there is recovery. The best is yet to be. A part of wisdom is not only to learn from the better contexts of our lives, but the poor, perhaps the bitter ones, as well – so to finish well our lives.

*Christmas with Arnie and sister in law Ann.*
*(Top) Tyler, Nathan (nephew)*
*(Bottom) Daniel (nephew), Aaron.*

# 12
# My Personal College

*"Real Christians ~~Don't~~ Dance."*
*John Fischer*

I didn't finish college. Counselors willing to dredge the past would likely tell me I should have. But I didn't. There was too much pulling, not pushing, me back home. I married, had children, worked at various jobs but lost my domestic and personal life context. My attitude and my faith have always been positive, and roused me from self-pity and a feeling of failure so to find in my work, my profession the fulfillment I craved – a fulfillment that all normal people feel to some degree. For some the matter is wistful, for others it becomes a driving force. For me it wasn't in excess but it was strong motivation. I went to work.

One of my first drives was to educate myself in the profession I loved. I had picked up the essentials from the years with various companies and from leaders that mentored me along – even demonstrating what not to do, how to function with respect for the context of order, earth, and human beings. I had the fundamentals, but I needed the maturity of solving the difficult problems.

I could make up for the lost college by dint of appreciation and courage. I always loved reading, a main conduct for learning, and I tend to remember what I read. My teachers were the people I found in my work – some of whom were sophisticated (well instructed in the field), and some who saw themselves as laborers (but able to do well their assignments). My gracious readers will permit me here to tell some of the story – the tale of my education to graduation and beyond. One can take control for a guided life at any year of life.

My life, like most lives has been visited by the ups and downs of both personal and professional experience. In a parade of experiences I, like others, was visited with both high animation and abysmal declension. I felt the joys and rewards of successes and the rejection and loss of the declines. I am told that the pattern is somewhat commonplace for most persons. When it happens the person may feel elevated with success and alone when the context has followed negative patterns. Rejection, real as interpreted so, is a painful, pressing factor in life. Some persons fall to depression, but all hope for a combination of vindication and reclusion against future disappointment. Can life be fixed to move always upward? Those that seek truthful answers to difficult questions will eventually be embraced by a reward that will create a deeper insight and responsibility leading to understanding of healthy, fulfilling and meaningful relationships. The truth is that the solutions are found by seeking both inside and outside ourselves perhaps to counselors, and for some to the creator who manages some matters so that He assists in gaining balance in life. He also revisits us with comfort and confidence by having us search for answers, and act on solutions. In the new century some of the best counselors have experienced divine contacts in their lives.

After Melody left our home in July, 1987, one of the terms of the divorce settlement was that she was willing to deed the house to me if I agreed to not oppose her objectives for the divorce. At the time it was an odd request, but I deduced that she was pregnant with the Doctor's child and felt she needed to re-marry before the birth. The doctor was a wealthy man and she had no need of our modest possessions. How I came to that conclusion is unclear to me even to this day.

I was serious about my reliance on faith factors so felt responsive to our preferences. Although uncomfortable and somewhat overcome, I prayed for direction and acceptance. I felt a deep malaise. Some days I was prayerful and sometimes on my own. It didn't always work out. I felt like a lost sheep, but also found. I had to press on. The sense of forced ambivalence came over me.

Even with this deep discomfort, I used some special insight to negotiate physical joint custody of our boys. Meaning they would stay with her for two weeks and then live with me for two weeks. In hind sight, I would have done this differently. This arrangement caused inconsistencies in assuring that all school work was completed. At the very least, the boys should have stayed at one of our homes during school days and the other during non-school days. This would have allowed stability in study habits, and balance for normality.

So it was that I, a lover of family, began my amended life as a single man. With the house in my possession, I brought in a renter to help offset the mortgage payment, and I needed a friend. Jim Ortiz was an apprentice electrician and lived quietly. We became good friends as we were both attempting to recover from divorces. Lonely and in need of companionship we would frequent the night life to offset the pain. That was not really an effective way to manage our problems and we did not continue the habit. It didn't really fit my value system.

All of this distraction began affecting my work and I soon began losing focus by not putting adequate energy into my vocation. I seemed like a different person, and was in some ways. After being released from Martin-McIntosh in early January, 1988, I went home overwhelmed and wept. My soul was paralyzed to a depth of depression that caused loss of functionality. Not only did I feel discarded by Melody but, in a few months, now my employer let me go. With her gone my identity was wrapped up in my profession, but that also was taken away. In the past I had dealt with disappointments but this was a double wallop that seemed unrepairable. For several days I floundered, suffering in self-pity. I just wanted to be alone. So I slept fitfully not wanting to do anything, or see anyone. I have been told the negative spirit and depression is a rather common combination during tunnel experiences of life. This was certainly a dark time for me. Persons going through these kinds of problems need to be ministered to by knowledgeable and empathetic persons. Many of us just 'tough-it-out.'

Ortiz noticed something wrong and contacted a friend, Cindy, who came over to see what she could do in my behalf. She sat at the foot of my bed in silence. She had that empathy and insight I needed. Cindy was the most compassionate and unselfish woman I had known to that point. Her remedy was to wait for her 'patient' to recover in his or own time. She had her own daemons that she had to overcome and had an insight into mine. She too was having trouble in her marriage. She seemed to understand the complexities. At least I was able to look directly into her face. For the first time in my life I felt as if someone actually could see into the inner depths of my being and did not hold me in contempt despite my faults. As she peered into my conflict she reminded me to embrace the pain, take over my life and never forget the feeling of triumph when it came. I will never forget her smile as I reiterated to her that, "Life is good." Nothing more was said as the phoenix rose from the ashes. I took on determination to emerge from the desperate funk that had visited me. I graduated from Cindy's school having conquered the self-despising of self-despair. Life seemed to emerge again for me.

My friends at the church knowing my situation did not call or check on me. Cindy and I dated and I decided to take a sabbatical from the church. This was ironic in that so much of my life was tied to church culture, but somehow it seemed the right thing to do.

After about a year, Cindy went back to her husband. However, we remained friends and maintained contact. She knew I enjoyed reading, so she introduced me two books "Real Christians Don't Dance!" and "Real Christians Don't Ask Why!" by John Fischer. These books challenged me to view Christianity in a fresh light and contributed to a new liberation of understanding my way in the world. My faith was strengthened in our reading and exchanges. Christianity is not a list of rules to follow but rather it is a relationship with our Creator. He is more interested in my sincerity and personal solutions than in my capabilities in my profession, or even in my family confusion. I was alone with his care for my life. This epiphany stays with me today and motivates me to a deeper connection with God who loves me. There is enough in Christian faith to carry any person submitting to his care.

Sometime after reading these books, Cindy called me and wanted me to meet Donna who later became my second wife. Shortly after Donna and I began dating, Donna was insistent that Cindy and I had to sever all contact. I reluctantly agreed understanding the problem of appearances. To this day I regret that decision because to me it had nothing to do with a romantic relationship but rather about having an insightful friend who could relate to my misery, and help me out of a dark tunnel. Donna expressed unyielding opinion about my temporary dependence. For her sake, I acquiesced. I have always felt some void for that loss because Cindy was the most forgiving and selfless person I have ever known. Her ideals had helped me in recovery. Recovery would have come faster if I could have followed through with her on her counsel. To this day conflict nags at me of the rights and wrongs of my life while reflecting on years gone by. Caught somewhere in the emotions of knowing what was wrong, felt so right. One can love a person deeply without the intimacy of marriage. Cindy died a few years ago and she is missed. She contributed so much to my life in matters of understanding and forgiveness. She was, for the time, God's gift to me. Out of this personal turmoil I learned that 'life must go on' – so make the most of it.

While at Martin-McIntosh, I had joined the local Bakersfield Chapter of the California Land Surveyors Association. My attendance at those monthly meetings meant I would become acquainted with several owners of other companies and one of those was Jerry VanCuren. He was Principal and owner of Simpson-Van Curen (SV). When I went to his office to give him my resume, he immediately recognized me. He informed me he would call me in a few days to let me know when I could begin work with his company. What a lift that was. Light was coming toward me in the tunnel.

My supervisor was Raul Gallo who was medium in stature with a Latino appearance. He had a mild temperament and very receptive to anyone with whom he engaged. My first assignment was to design a mile long road in the hilly sections of northeast Bakersfield. I found out that we were behind schedule and this was a rush job. Using my construction staking experience of dealing with slopes and grades I was able to demonstrate to Gallo my abilities to both design and work on an assignment under time constraints. I loved the challenge.

Gallo declared confidence in my work and schedule. He assigned me to the staking of this road.

For my chainman he gave me a 'seasoned' elderly man with over 35 years of experience as a chainman. Don Langley's appearance was one that could have easily been in a spaghetti western alongside Clint Eastwood. His actions complimented his gnarly appearance. One day after leaving a restaurant he poured a full packet of sugar into a Styrofoam cup of ice tea.

Unfortunately, he forgot to bring a spoon to stir the drink. Improvising he reached into the back of the work truck and pulled out a rusty railroad spike and proceeded to mix the ingredient. My reaction was along the lines of: 'Don! Really!' His reply was: "Ahh, it won't hurt nothing." He is the only person I have known enjoying rusty tea. On another occasion, as he was about to enter a hospital for treatment of a heart attack, he surmised they would not permit smoking in the hospital so he simply had to have a cigarette in the parking lot before entering the emergency room. His reasoning was it could be his last one. It wasn't.

He never desired to rise to the level of party chief and was quite content in his position. He had an innate ability to sense a problem and would quickly inform me when something did not look right. After a few calculations, I determined he was correct and something was amiss. I learned quickly to listen when he spoke and not pass him off in cavalier fashion. I deeply appreciated him and he is a character in my life that shaped my view of the structure of field crews and the need for all participants to be engaged. It becomes extremely important to comprehend the dynamics of field staff. Today the surveyor is tempted to operate a 'one-man' crew due to the sophistication of survey equipment and subject to the skill and willingness to operate alone. There is something to be said about placing a second pair of eyes on the projects. I was learning nearly every day some new concept or procedure.

Another employee at SV was Matt Gilligan who was and is extremely detailed with a yearning for perfection – a useful trait for surveyors. I found him to be both supporting and frustrating at the same time. For the first few days he would tell me that things weren't fitting together and we had a problem. Soon I learned that my acceptance level could be different from others. His happened to be extremely rigid almost to the level of impossibility for performance. However, he was a very engaging fellow and we soon became good friends - even to this day. With Gilligan everything had to be more than right.

He later came to work for me when I first started my business. Often times we would go out on the night life where he attempted to teach me how to dance to country music - but to no avail. He was a very good dancer – clearly unlike me. To this day I have never been able to catch the beat in any type of music. That seems peculiar for athletes, but it is standard for me. However, my ear can pick out the separate instruments being played in a musical performance. What Gilligan was to math I was to music, if the focus was on the refinement of action and numbers.

Tim Smith was the other party chief for SV. His father was a surveyor and well respected within the community. Smith was probably the best note keeper I have ever encountered. The biggest attribute was that they were legible unlike mine. He would take his time and make sure he had all the details. This is important because often times months go by and the surveyor will have to recall the events from the field notes. Unless they have extremely good memory, the emerging matter can become extremely problematic. Notes, when recorded properly, can save a lot of time and money. Not only was I enjoying working with these men, I was learning. I made my contribution to them by making the best use of the skills I saw in them.

Later Smith came to work for me. He was sporting a full beard and mustache. He would joke that he had his beard since he was eight years of age. While interviewing for a position, I informed him that we worked for an oil company that would not allow beards for safety reasons. The logic for the rule was that a mask would not fit properly should there arise a need for it to be worn in an emergency situation. He reluctantly agreed and would shave his beard the day he had to go in the oil patch and grow it back until the next oil trip. Through all of it, he proved a valuable asset to the profession. Part of the satisfaction I have gained from being a surveyor relates to the fellows with whom I have worked, and from whom I have learned so much. We were strong friends in the respect we shared in the work we did.

Life was beginning to take a turn for the better with good friends and co-workers who made it all interesting. Life brightened. It got even better when I found out that I had passed the State exam and would soon receive a full license to practice Land Surveying in California. I had a document acknowledging that I knew enough to be trusted both in knowledge and performance. For me this became my college degree. My teachers were the interesting men with whom I worked. I was now the principal of the school. Obtaining that license was a huge morale booster and instilled in me a confidence that I had a calling. It symbolized the assurance of worth in a world that so often rejects and sets aside those in personal, private conflict. More importantly it instilled in me a compassion for those who are striving to find their place in the world. Gifts and talents are granted to all in different shapes and sizes. The challenge to each person is to unearth what they are and can become in circumstances that would suppress discovery. We need to have the courage to keep going, even in the dark periods. The light will come on. Past detours will be memories for learning. I have a collegiate professor friend who informed me that many college graduates never learn these necessary life lessons.

Soon after obtaining my license I was sent to work on Military Bases in California. Most of the work was to locate utility boxes and paint them so that they could be identified in an aerial photograph. The management entailed painting each utility with a different symbol so that water could be distinguished from sewer and sewer could be recognized from gas valves, and so forth. This too is the work of surveyors. It is the part of making modern life safe in our accident prone modern society.

While at these bases I soon learned that security was more important than the work I was doing. My first encounter was with a female Marine Sargent at the 29 Palms entrance gate. She had a persuasive authoritarian confidence that aroused a nervous disposition and uncertainty for me. As I fumbled through the paper work, she stood stoically waiting for me to gather my wits. After a few moments, I finally acknowledged how she made me nervous to which I thought I saw a faint smile of satisfaction. Apparently recognition of her authority is what she wanted to communicate. I may have given her the gift she wanted. I am unsure what it was.

On another occasion, our truck was part of a random search where we had to unload all items in the work truck. This was a daunting task in that our truck was loaded with flagging, lathe, nails, wood stakes, tripods, etc. Many of the items are loosely carried and scattered. It took us well over an hour to accommodate but supervisors were diligent and insistent. That incident was embarrassing and caused me to reflect on the time as a child I went to the doctor and wasn't wearing underwear. From that point on it convinced me that a survey truck needs to be well organized. My time on these bases caused me to respect and gain an understanding of the importance of discipline along with orderly conduct. It was another lesson that made me do better next time. It contributed to a sense of respect for what I was doing and compliments for jobs well done. The principal needed to go to graduate 'classes' from time to time – sometimes learning what should have been known and practiced all along the way.

When I wasn't at Military Bases, I was in Bakersfield conducting surveys and often had to be in the middle of heavy traffic. It would often become quite precarious with cars and semis zooming past at breakneck speeds. The "Survey Crew Ahead" signs and cones only seemed to encourage nefarious acts of alarm such as honking when they were next to the workers just to see how it affected us. It was as if they felt they owned the road and we had no right to be there. We have to be gracious enough to blame it on humanity: It's only human, to be mean.

During those days technology had advanced so that we could use Electronic Distance Meters which allowed us to measure distances of up to two miles. In these situations communication was a must but proved difficult when the walkie-talkies were not functioning properly. When they didn't we would have to resort to plan B which meant using various forms of signals such as hands, lights, or mirrors reflecting the sun. For example we would wave our hands or flash the beams on the truck when the measurement was completed. It is a marvelous system, but it can become problematic – humanity again.

I learned from an amateur the importance of having a seasoned chainman especially when I was on a busy road. Jess was retired mechanic and a good friend of Mr. Van Curen. Jess just wanted to get out and do something different so I took him with me on a 'short' job that required that we work in the middle of a very busy Highway. We had only two points to set so I thought we could get in and out quickly. My instructions were for him to go down the middle of the Highway about 600 feet and turn the glass portion of the prism to me so I could get a reading on the distance. Initially first I had to get him on the line I wanted so I radioed in a professional voice: "Right a foot." Instead he went left to which I responded "The other Right." After gaining that shift I calculated that he was five feet short and needed to go further. I instructed him that he needed to take a couple of steps back: "Go Away five feet." However, his stance was facing at right angles to me so instead of walking five more feet away from me he moved the prism from his perspective, himself which was different from mine. My back was in a different direction than his. My next command was simply to gain some correction: "Left five feet and go away from me five more feet." And so the follies continued until the radios ceased to function. In this case being under extreme pressure from traffic and the need to complete the job, Jess became visibly anxious - as was I. Thinking there was only two points, I gave my 'helper' a quick lesson on hand signals. The problem is that these signals can be seemingly complicated to the novice especially when he was under duress. We eventually placed the points but I learned a valuable lesson in when to use unlearned assistants and when not to. Such lessons reduce irresistible exasperation.

After some time working at SV, I was promoted to the position of Chief of Parties meaning I would schedule and set up the field crews. My duties were enlarged. This position allowed me to learn the important aspects of interacting with clients and project coordinators. My position also permitted me to give cost proposals for prospective projects which most of the time was for construction staking. I learned very quickly that the key was not to get the job at any price but rather find that fine line where a reasonable profit can be made. Over the years, I have come to the conclusion that construction staking requires a great deal of time and energy to accommodate sometimes a great number of people. Some invariably believe it costs less than it does for a project. When laying out plans and sites for buildings, the responsibilities and obligations we must go to not only the General Contractor who is overseeing the project but also to the sub-contractors as well. There are so many persons involved expecting to finance their contributions with various requirements that may not be known. Sometimes the amount of subs on a project may number twenty or more workers which would include the grader, the guy who is constructing the bolts for the columns, the concrete contractor, the carpenter, HVAC person, plumber, electrician, and the list goes on. The point is that construction staking can bring with it a potentially huge liability as well as highly competitive bidding processes. Many times these proposals can be ridiculously low. Competition can become destructive. No wonder so many contractors go broke. The horizon is strewn with them – the bidders that are too low for the cost of the projects.

In this new assignment I did find that this arena of land surveying could bring with it instant increase in workload. The problem is that the profit line could be minimal and sometimes lose money, so to hope to make up the loss on the next project. The other pit fall is dealing with plans that were prepared by other companies, plans we may not have had any past in making. These plans often will have nuances that are not readily explained and can be subject to variant interpretations. This causes excuses and reactions such as; "We laid it out according to the plans" - when problems occurred. This may be true but the larger question was disregarded. Did it relieve the new professional or groups from project responsibility? The new people sense that the former people had reneged when they discovered the poor bidding that launched the project. In my opinion technicians do as they are told while the true professional engages in attempting to correct short-comings of the project. Through the years I have arrived at to the conclusion that the surveyor should be retained by the owner and not inserted into a line item by the contractor. It becomes a loyalty factor in that the surveyor, or anybody else, will tend to accommodate the one who is paying the bill. The industry is adjusting to find the best way to order its projects. The owner will likely benefit in the quality of the completed contract.

I am grateful to SV, particularly to Jerry Van Curen for his patience and tutelage on the inner workings of the proposals, contracts, time lines, completion, and billings. This experience was incredibly valuable in assisting me through the years of my own business. I was gaining invaluable experience to assure success for launching on my own. I was near my graduation day, but didn't think of my experience as similar to a college graduation.

On one particular day Mr. Van Curen walked into my office at around 4:30 in the afternoon and informed me that they just received a new set of plans for a project on Sillect Avenue in Bakersfield. The drawings available changed the location of the building under construction. This meant we would have to go back to the site and move the stakes to the new location. The problem for us was that they wanted to begin construction the next morning. Because we already had scheduled the crews elsewhere, Van Curen and I would have to visit the site to move the stakes. Van Curen had not worked in the field for several years and I got the impression that he wanted to get back to it even if only for a few hours. Surveyors tend to love nature and prefer to work in it – rather than in stuffy offices. I was putting on life together with knowledge of my assignments, patience with people, practice in evaluations, willing for the extra effort, and loving the challenge of it all.

The next morning we met at the site to which I pulled the tripod out of the back of the truck and attached the instrument to it. He grabbed the tripod and instrument and proceeded to place them over the control point. As I was preparing the notes and gathering material, I looked over at him and noticed that he had a plumb bob in his hand and was looking puzzled at the underside of the tripod head to which he asked with frustration; "Who took the hook off of the bottom of the tripod?" I replied "I did." "Why did you do that? How are you going to set it up over the point if you don't have something to hang the plumb bob from?" It was then that I realized it had been a long time since he had been in the field and I certainly did not want to embarrass him, so I thought carefully how to answer his inquiry. After all he was my boss and respect was rightfully due him. And, it might make some difference for me.

"We don't need to use the plumb bob, we can see the point from the optical plummet. If you will look through this eyepiece on the side of the instrument you will be able to see the point on the ground. You look through the eyepiece and move and adjust the legs until the circle is directly over the point"

He peered through the eyepiece and leaned back, looked at me and said, "Interesting." The 'ol timer' experienced several of the newer procedures quite different from a couple decades earlier.

We finished setting the last stake just as the contractor was driving up. We explained to the contractor the change and drove back to the office. It was a job well done with touching generations.

My boss may not have been current with the latest technology, but he still had the poise and dignity to utilize those that did. That day I gained a new respect for him and obtained a valuable lesson on the art of delegation. (Besides, I knew where my pay check came from.)

During my days at SV I learned that rejection can be dissipated and that although one may feel rebuffed and rejected for the moment there are new friends and relationships awaiting. I had a ways to go before I sleep. There is recovery.

In November, 1991, Donna and I married and that followed by a honeymoon aboard a cruise ship to the Bahamas. As work began to slow down at SV and I was beginning a new family, Donna and I began discussing the idea of venturing into a Land Surveying business. We wanted to control our own destiny. In April, 1992, we officially opened for business from our kitchen counter top. We were on our way to a new adventure that would span over 25 years and that has made all the difference. I was a bit late, but not too late. My education had been gained in the field. I had recovered from personal troubles, gaining lessons both human and spiritual. I knew the future would be better structured. I felt determined, thankful – and on my way. The lessons of life in forgiveness and courage, in relief from self-doubt, in learning my craft, in the graduation from the school of experience, and documents proving my 'completion' of basic studies, I was ready – and the vision worked.

*Grandma Nelms and Me, at Mom and Dad's ranch in Orland, CA.*
*She had numerous Grandchildren, but I was her favorite. At least she made*
*me feel that way. Speaking to my cousins & siblings, they argue that they*
*were her favorite. She made us all feel that way.*

# 13
# Life to Legacy

*"Glory of God to conceal, glory of kings to search."*
Proverbs

C.S. Lewis, of Oxford University fame in scholarship, and Church reputation for his aggressive Christian faith and literary life, wrote his popular autobiography "Surprised by Joy" and closed it on his 29th year, less than half the years he lived. He died on the cusp of retirement on the same day that President Kennedy was shot in Texas. As a young man at 29 years, he may have felt that his public life thereafter would speak for itself, for the reality of his favorable public reputation in the world. He chose that transitional year because he wanted to change his personal life to fit his recent commitment to the Christian faith which not only included life and thought changes, but the sense of direction for his life. Life in the world context would be changed for him and for others by his future and influence. People would be seen and accepted in the light of spiritual maturation. Even his professional life would be amended to advance Christian ministry to mankind. He lived to become famous and revered beyond any achievement he might have conjured before his conversion. Part of his success appears to have been in his deep understanding and imagination related to the parable contexts of life from the Bible, modern everyday life, and imaginative literature. We will return to Lewis at the close of this chapter and current purpose for my life and family – and relationship with professional life quest.

My life was not on similar patterns of accomplishments as those of Lewis but like him I want to close my story at the point where I believe I have matured in the whole of my generation. I began my professional life in my mid-twenties and some would say later than I should have found it, but it did emerge and will continue well, if my energy holds. I have been assured that I found the area for which I was truly suited – even if it was preceded by a lot of poling around – with hits and misses. Had I accepted the discipline of completing my college education, my course direction would have been clearer and easier - much earlier. My decision to marry while very young and distracted by romance, I would likely have had matters in better order. I lost that family in the decline of our marriage, but I pressed on and also lost the second attempt to build a family. Separation and divorce were not my preference. The family efforts and omissions make up the greatest disappointment in my adult life but I learned the lessons that must have been intended for the loss, and have found excellent relationship with my sons and their growing families that warms my life. What a treasure they are to me. I have taken the clues that my personal success is found in regarding and helping others. This has led to caring and magnificent friendships especially with persons who enjoy personal service in professional life. It means that I not only have emerged in a successful business and service, but fulfilling in the influence of life formation. This includes the meaning for life and the faith that completes the objectives of life experience and makes effective contributions. This leadership in and to the professional and public groups for advancing social life and improving society seems like a gift to me. All the serious persons I have known seem to want to give back to a wonderful world and life privilege.

I perceive such an attitude as a gift from God. The failures and successes have been accepted as necessary to find wisdom for the rest of life – with both satisfaction and pleasure that belongs to maturity and fulfillment.

In the meantime, I need to bring my readers, friends, and family up-to-date on my life and vision as I interpret maturity. Some persons and colleagues have wondered about my response to my life events. Maturity to mankind leads to wisdom, a god–like factor for human beings. Too few of us search for it. I was late to the process. The recitation of my life story is part of my process – so to focus on the wisdom process. I am grateful to have found fulfillment in large and small strokes.

Obtaining a License to practice Land Surveying in California gave a euphoric feeling of accomplishment and instilled a sense of professional arrival. It gave me the self-assurance that I had found my gift and a sense of self-worth while standing amongst peers. This was attained through repetitive successes and a determination to acquire professional goals. It took considerable time but emerged during the years to the point of invitation to professional peer leadership.

However, having an official license to practice a professional discipline does not necessarily equate to survival in a business setting. I was determined to succeed in the work I loved and felt called to do. I had hoped for family participation, but each member found a different route. We have a right to form our ways.

Soon after our wedding in November of 1991 work began to slow down at Simpson-VanCuren. Donna and I began discussing the idea of starting our own survey company. Bakersfield College was offering, through their business institute, a short six week course on how to start a small business. Small business is generally perceived to be key to American economy's success. This became obvious with strong conviction by analysts during the virus pandemic of 2020.

Enrolling, I went to the first class where the instructor walked to the head of a class of about forty people and introduced himself. Then pausing for affect he asked how many wanted to start a business because they wanted to be their own boss? Over thirty people raised their hands. Then he asked how many wanted to be in business because they want to set their own hours? The same people raised their hands. Then he said: "You are in it for the wrong reasons and are destined for failure because you will not be your own boss and you will not be able to set your own hours."

He gave the illustration of preparing to be on your way for a day at Disneyland with your family when a call comes in that the pipes in the walk-in freezer broke in your restaurant. You now have to decide whether you shut the business down until you get back or do you fix the problem. Prof then went on to explain the importance of establishing a business plan and a budget. His example was very sobering to consider and caused me to reflect on why I wanted to start any endeavor. My reasons had to be truthful and I had to understand that they would own me. Many start–ups fail for this lack of full dedication. I felt I could make my dedication to duty. I wanted to be a surveyor. I would pay the price.

After careful consideration, we decided to take the plunge. Our first investment was the purchase of a fax machine. Before the age of the internet, fax machines were a must in order for information to get out quickly. The cost at the time for this type of machine was around $600 which was a significant investment; at least for us. Donna and I agreed that we should go for it.

Soon we were sending out proposals to contractors for construction jobs. We made a self-imposed condition that if we received at least $10,000 in contracts in the first month then we would continue. Two days before the deadline we received two contracts to stake a K-Mart site in Kingsburg and a Walmart in Selma totaling over $20,000. Soon after that I received a contract for an Albertsons in Ridgecrest and another Walmart in Lompoc. We maxed out our credit cards in the tune of $20,000 to acquire needed supplies. However, it did not include a much needed $7,000 instrument that was vital for measuring distances and turning angles. Our attempt to gain a small business loan was thwarted due to the fact that technically I did not have a job. A vendor in Ventura, Lewis & Lewis, hearing of my plight agreed to grant me a twelve month lease agreement with a $1 buyout after one year for the instrument. Through the years I have been forever grateful and devoted my loyalty to them because they took a chance on me but did not personally profit from it. I would like to believe I would mentor a person as committed as I was in the work and planning. I am informed that nearly all dedicated persons, to a project are assisted by those able to inspire start-ups – because they too were assisted long before.

Working out of our home and needing an office to perform calculations, we set up the kitchen countertop as a drafting station. Each night I would put all my work to the side so we could prepare dinner. After a few months we purchased a drafting table and turned the garage into an office. So began our quest in the surveying business. It grew and became viable until we bought a building and even drew tenants trying to reach their dreams professionally. We wanted to serve while being served.

With just over ten years of experience under some excellent surveyors and leaders, I felt I could handle all these projects but it became increasingly evident that I was not making adequate profit – no more than mere sustainability. After the first month, I realized I was only making about $3/hour as the owner. Employees were doing better. Inexperience and lack of business knowledge ate into the profit margin. I soon realized what a "mark-up" was. Just because the material costs one dollar does not mean I should charge the client in the same price. There was also the purchase of insurance policies for cars and trucks, workman's compensation, and liability agreements – as well as equipment. In addition, I had to hire someone to assist me in the field which leads to not only wages but withholding taxes and increased paper work. Those withholding taxes had to be paid right away or severe fines would be placed on the business. I had a lot to learn from the business side and knew I had to adjust quickly. My education occurred at the time it was required in the moment. Surveying was natural for me. Business decisions were 'tougher.' I studied experience and it worked.

In addition, I soon realized that I was going to have difficulty meeting time schedules dictated by the various projects. Feeling it my duty to fulfill my contractual obligations and with no working capital, I worked 16 hour days. For a period of time I was going 20 hours a day seven days a week. Typical day was getting up at 4 in the morning to travel 90 miles north of Bakersfield to

Kingsburg. Work until 10pm by car headlights then make the trip back to Bakersfield to sleep four hours then head 90 miles east to Ridgecrest and work late into the evening; followed by rising the next morning at 4am to a 120 mile trip west to Lompoc for an all-day staking request and back home; followed the next day by a 100 mile trek north to Selma. I had a lot to learn about over committing in business, and under committing to family. But somehow I met my obligations, and got away with it because I liked the field. Without that motivation I would likely have failed in business.

Even though they were long days, I attempted to draw family in with the work. Some families have outings that entail trips to the ocean, camping, or amusement parks; but our family would choose a trip to Wal-Mart. One would think that it is not necessarily a bad outing if we were to go shopping. Our trip was not to shop but to set construction stakes. Excitement for me might not be the same for the children. They were obedient to my professional needs, with a moan here or there. I recite here just one of the family 'outings' on the job. It remains in my memory to illustrate the effort I wanted to make to turn my professional work into family togetherness. Even though it didn't really succeed, it did leave one with memories of my family ideals.

We acquired a contract to stake a new Wal-Mart in Fresno which was about 90 miles from where we lived. Our contract was almost complete except for the staking of the parking lot. Donna and I discussed it and thought why not take the family. A family conference was assembled and it was decided that we would go on Friday after school, arrive at the sight work a few hours, stay the night, get up early Saturday and finish the project by noon. This would leave us the opportunity to spend the rest of the day visiting my mother-in-law who lived nearby. The boys were excited because they were going to get some money for their efforts (which was more than I was getting) and visit grandma who lived in a rural area where they could shoot their BB guns.

We arrived at the sight on Friday evening and gave instructions. All went well Friday night, although we did not complete as much as I would have liked, but we would get up early Saturday and finish it.

Sometimes I can be a naïve father and believe that my children have the greatest of enthusiasm as I do for completing projects and going to do something just for fun. Reality set in and my hopes were dashed when the boys were lazily attending to their assignments. The event turned into a continuous barrage of coaxing techniques that ranged from the words "please" to the extremely stern warnings of punishment. It ended in threats of calling the outing to Gramma's postponed to a later date.

I would ask Tyler to hold zero of the tape over the control point to which he struggled as if he had just finished a marathon race and was ready to collapse. Aaron's response to my request to bring me the hub bag was as if he were climbing to the peak of Mount Everest in desperate need of oxygen. (The boys just were not cut out to be surveyors.)

It should have dawned on me that my boys were not blessed with any love for surveying. Life for them was not working together, but playing together at least some of the time, the time they would remember. We finally finished our task that day and I informed them that we were complete. They asked if they could investigate a curious tractor on the site. I gave them the nod. They perked up. Suddenly life took on a different view. They didn't seem to be tired or called to duty.

Their recovery from the fatigue and strain was no less than miraculous, somewhere along the line of the parting of the Red Sea or the raising of the lame man to walk. They immediately dropped everything and sprinted to the machine that sat a few hundred yards away. Donna and I just looked at each other in mock surprise at the sudden burst of energy and improved personality.

A few minutes later we had everything loaded in the truck to which I called the boys to interrupt their latest activity where they were using four foot wood lathe as swords. The fight was vigorous and enthusiastic. A second call was made with the threat they were going to be left behind if they did not come quickly, which inspired a swift foot race back to the truck that would have impressed world class sprinters. Miracles of miracles are witnessed every day in families and mine was no different.

I look back at those grueling days with fondness as a time that I could include the boys and teach them the importance of a good work ethic. Many a time I would take them and they seemed to enjoy the experience. Although they did not become surveyors, they found their own path in life as we all must do. There was real value for them in developing a work ethic, but I may have missed my duty in other ways in developing a family I wanted and worked so hard to gain. It isn't all serious stuff.

Today the business continues on and proceeds well. The story continues and although it is not about the one who 'hit the big time' and how he got there, it is rather a story about the average person attempting to find their gift in life for achievement. Hopefully the reader is inspired to self search to understand early in life who they are and the gifts that lie within them. A major reason I write this memoir is to challenge readers to find the gifts that God has given to all to achieve within for the balance in life we were meant to gain.

Looking back, I am forever grateful to those who nudged me in the right direction. Especially to those mentors who found the time to nurture my abilities. They recognized that we all have talents and gifts that long to emerge and demonstrate themselves. My hope is that I would replicate their patience and encouragement to others to find their own way. I want to serve others as they served me. To me, one of the main tenets of life is that we serve each other. You see it in Scripture and in service clubs such as Rotary. That makes givers and receivers of all normal persons. The pattern is followed in love and humility. My peers have elected me to offices I never thought would come to me. In this the opportunity to serve and mentor others have expanded. The story is motivating.

This chapter began with the half auto-bio story of C.S. Lewis. He wanted to tell what preceded the greatest story that formed his new and animated life of maturing as a Christian human being.

Although I do not compare myself with him in intellect, he did have many similar experiences to mine with others in growing up, of education and breaking experiences like when he served as a front-line soldier in the British military during World War I. All this incorporated the trials and errors that included carnality and distractions of youth of the generation. He found little peace in any trial transition. He settled into the life of a University Don, dedicated to the formation of students. He remained unmarried until near the end of life, then only to suffer in the depths of grief and resistance in the death of his wife. In her closing months she ministered unto him. It became an entrancing story in an Academy Award cinema seen by millions throughout the World. He wrote a best-seller book about his decline and recovery during the ordeal. So I have written my story of gain and loss in the story of life, and will use my life to encourage others to find the joy of accomplishment even in some defeats, large and small.

So I arrive at this point in the course of my life with joy, achievement and faith but also disappointment marking the years. It is likely that I am at the acme of my professional life with first class assignments in a California central city. It fulfills my childhood dreams and imagination about activity in open nature. It seemed that the profession found me. I find fulfillment in it. That has been recognized by others who have contracts with our company and have elected my name to head public and professional organizations. Further my faith life has added values, maturity and graces to my days that would not have occurred without participation and involvement of my mentors. I have no negative feelings about any person or groups of persons. I repeat myself: We were born to live to help one another in the challenging life of humanity. The concept is Christian, although seldom credited to western origin commonly communicated in history.

Although my relationship with my sons has become beautiful carrying over into their families, my marriages have been distracted with other interests, perhaps with some omissions on the part of either of us in two relationships. The first broken by the common distraction of one person drawn to a preferred benefit of building a different life with someone during our formation years. The second situation was likely lost in the various hobbies that did not fit the lives of both husband and wife. I have peace so that I hold no ill will toward anyone related to my life, near or far. The days now long gone by are remembered for making me a lover of life, colleagues, family and friends. There is a bit of elevation in it that overcomes the negatives. Forgiveness makes the good parts into memories and the poor into forgetfulness. I am pleased for my children and grandchildren. They have provided to my legacy in family. I could not have known how fulfilling that could be until it happened. The best is yet to be for those who find fulfillment in faith, family, formation and service to mankind. It is comforting to find good will for all persons in this wonderful life to be sought and found.

So it is that I have arrived at the golden years of my life doing what I do best. I am full of appreciation for persons who helped me along the way. I have rejected my negative life experiences except to have learned from them so to encourage others especially my grandchildren. I expect to live out my life well, and my hope is that my story will encourage the reader to pursue the talents that have been gifted to them and live your live well. It is not an easy challenge, for as the Proverb reminds me "It is the glory of God to conceal and it is the glory of kings to search." Seek with all your heart and stay the path, for your reward will be far more than you ever expected as you put the Big Sticks by the Little Sticks.

*Dad and I at San Francisco Giants game in 2013. We shared a commonality in following the Giants since I was a lad.*

# 14

# Putting Big Sticks by Little Sticks

*"That's a lot of acronyms."*
*Joe Tallman*

Historians' research and record rather fully, the biographies and achievements of men and women who, in their venturesome spirits and passions set out to find what may be found beyond the seas or behind the mountains- east and west, north and south. Some were driven by commerce and perhaps personal wealth; some by discovery, perhaps routes to distant lands; some by love of country, perhaps conquest; some to find a better life than they knew, perhaps a fountain of youth; some to spread their religion, likely Christianity, perhaps for the grace of God; and, some for adventure, perhaps to carry out a sovereign's command. All of them had to utilize, to greater or lesser degree, learnings in mathematics and science to achieve great objectives for mankind. Even so, there had to be some fire from within that we call motivation and desire.

They charted continents and seas to identify routes to peoples and places different from their own. In the process they proved or disproved theories of what lay beyond the known world of their era. They projected ideas and theories about unknowns, and presumed problems to be solved by future venturing in imaginative projects. Much of it was done with few tools, perhaps a compass and sexton, emerging a remarkable ability to chart lands and shores with more or less accuracy. Those men and women were usually practical in the risks, but also visionary and adventuresome. Some were cavaliers but advancing world knowledge even when they were not aware of the negative sides to their ventures. Adventure remains in our era, greatly advanced by improved means for accuracy, for creative avenues, and a sense of fulfillment in the measurement of creation relating to truth about the natural world. There is inspiration and achievement in the process for those willing to give important life to it. This is an adventurous creative life for any person paying the price for it. It makes creation organized for mankind.

During the late 13th century, Marco Polo, the son of a Venetian merchant, travelled extensively from Italy to inner Asia. His motivation was a two pronged attempt to stop the Mongol incursions in Europe and convert inhabitants to Christianity. His book titled in the prologue Le Divisament dou Monde (The Description of the World), better known to English students as The Travels of Marco Polo, became a source of cartographic information and influenced Martin Behaim (1459-1507) to develop a globe called the Erdapfel (Earth Apple). Behaim was trusted for his scientific knowledge particularly in exploration and cartography. However, his globe was severely flawed in that it showed Japan only 80 degrees west of the Canary Islands and China only 35 degrees further west.

However, even with the flaws there was pointing in progress directions, and the challenge to verify or correct the lines and theories so to set the stage for meaningful study of earth and water to better the lives of human beings. Management of the earth by persons relates to exploration and order in such charting and identification. Measurement of land and sea masses began. In this there is responsibility and advancement, in discovery and preservation for purpose. Those that participated in the challenge moved on in what we call civilization. Those who did not engage were limited to minimal life and circumstances. This is observed significantly in the American Indian informality about the ordering of land rights, and the incursion of the Caucasians to measure and, by documentation, legally order land distribution, so to determine responsibility for it. Those taking the matter seriously ended up with ownership and control.

Many historians believe the earth globe and the Polo's, Divisament, sparked Christopher Columbus' theory that Japan was only 2,400 nautical miles from the Canary Islands. In reality it is four times that distance. After the Portuguese rejected his request for support, Columbus went to the Spanish monarchs; Isabella and Ferdinand, for funding and commission. Through persistence and argument he convinced them that he may have hit upon a shorter trade route to Asia than circumvention by way of South Africa. A shorter route would expedite commerce and reduce costs. In a growing spirit of expansion and trade, perhaps conquest, rising in European nations, and taken together with yearnings for shorter trade routes, Spain approved the proposal of the Italian, Columbus. He found a way to the unknown western half of the world. We now know what they summarize as the rest of the story is history. (The Viking sorties earlier were not recorded or followed through. With Columbus the move began to go west.)

Sailing westward in behalf of Spain and the mission of the Church, Columbus used a compass for direction, sand clock for time, and speed by eye calculation with the stars- so to arrive on an island which Columbus believed was the shore of India. In actuality he went ashore on an island in the Caribbean, just south of what is now the United States. It wasn't long until the informed populations gave up flat earth theories for global concepts. (Even in our time period there are person holding out for a flat earth. They can't seem to grasp the math, the geometry that if a globe is large enough it seems flat to the standing individual.) The globe is so large, and the curvature so modest that the earth seems flat to our experience.

With nearly all the world populations believing that the earth's circumference to be smaller than it really is (25,000 miles in circumference at the Equator), Ferdinand Magellan, in 1520, set out to discover a passage around the southern tip of South America. Enduring hardships extending from freezing temperatures to crew insubordination, he discovered the strait that later bore his name. Slowly, he sailed across the Pacific becoming aware, in a voyage carried through in extreme circumstances, that he had covered about a third of the earth's surface. Even though his venture proved that the long passage was impractical for trade, his crew's circumvention of the globe, by water, inspired others to romanticize the search for uncharted lands, shorter routes, and unknown areas. The world became a reality in all directions and in its totality, largely to be exploited in some way by nations with power and organization as they began to seek out distant shores for colonization and wealth. The measurement of the globe was under way beginning with national claims on it – in colonization. We may not perceive, in our time, how this information amazed the nations - especially of Europe. It would be equivalent to our feelings when the American space ship, the Eagle, landed on the moon. That becoming normal to us seemed almost a miracle to them. What nation can claim the property of the moon?

The 16th Century is often termed as the Age of Discovery. A major contributor to world exploration and travel was Gerard Mercator. He was not an explorer nor was he a world traveler but his accomplishments changed the way the world was viewed. He was the son of a cobbler but was raised to prominence as one of the premier map makers of all time. He is best known for the naming of the Americas and his ability to project lines from a globe to a flat map surface. He named the Americas after another searcher of earth dimensions, Amerigo Vespucci. In 1501,

Vespucci, sailed south of the equator from five degrees to thirty degrees along the coast of what is today Brazil. He concluded that this was a previously unknown continent, so a New World – a name that has also stuck for the movement from Europe to the west in the Americas so that the west became the New World. He is now remembered in the names of North and South America. The call for measurement was becoming more insistent. What in South America was to be claimed by the Spanish and what by the Portuguese? Neighbors in Europe, they became neighbors in South America. The Spanish measured the land into a number of separated countries, and the Portuguese decided on one, Brazil. Today's languages in South America continue the division of the early conquistadors – with several small Spanish speaking nations and one large Portuguese. (Even after the passing centuries several extreme boundaries remain in dispute for some Spanish speaking areas.) Where measurement has been uncertain, even in our time, disputes and land management has been difficult. Arguments continue related to some borders of countries in South America in the jungle areas.

Even though it was an era of discovery it was also an age of some inquisition. Vested Church authorities tended to resist learning they did not originate, or approved before knowledge dissemination. Mercator had adapted so to avoid Church heresy with his maps. He proposed a new world mapping in the shape of a heart to acknowledge creation in a pattern that he believed would illustrate God's sovereignty. Viewing his maps as an expression of himself, he developed them with imaginative adaptation. The charting stimulated explorers with desire to investigate the world. Explorers are well known like: Hernando de Soto, who explored the Mississippi River Valley; Francis Drake, who explored the west coast of North America; Vizcaino, exploring from Gosnold to Buzzards Bay; Pring and Weymouth, exploring New England; and, Henry Hudson exploring the east coast of North America – to name a few.

These penetrations in turn prompted settlers in the 17th century to relocate in the new found lands, some for cavalier reasons or religious objectives and others to start a new life. Present day Newfoundland was named in this spirit of finding new lands. (The lands had been there all the while with sparse human populations, Indians. There was a sense in which the lands were discovering the invaders.) The melting pot concept of new societies was at a beginning, even though splintered, and slow moving at first. It was something that emerged in the new lands, almost non-existent in the Old World. It would flourish in the nineteenth century – spilling into the twentieth century, and becoming more world-wide. (However, Nations like Russia were reaching out to the unknown. In the Russian effort the area known as Alaska was occupied. Some of the Russian culture can still be found there. In those days Russians built Christian Chapels in explored lands. Some evidences of them remain.)

In the 18th century Captain James Cook sailed throughout the Pacific in search for trade routes to India, China, and Japan. His other assignment was to search for a third land mass called Terra Australis Incognita sometimes known as the Southern Continent. Supposedly it lay somewhere in the southern Pacific Ocean. The belief was that in order for the earth to have balance with the other two hemispheres it 'had to be triune' since "God was triune!" Cook set sail to find this mystic land. With coordinates in hand, he proved that there was no such land mass, forcing the prevailing church authority to re-evaluate its theological presumption and model of creation. Trinity is not found in everything. However, the concepts invited crews to the whole world to verify theories. Many of those theories fell to better understanding of the earth and seas. An underlying belief in God was one of the motivations for exploration, so to honor the whole world as known to God's people. Columbus wrote about the matter of Christian objectives with people of new lands.

The search for the Northwest Passage became an obsession for England in the early to mid-1800s. With much fan fair the English launched John Franklin's state of the art ships – after sailing never to be heard from again. It was during the search of Franklin that the route of passage was discovered but it proved to be an impractical trade route. Currently, the effort continues encouraged by the shrinking Arctic ice. Russia now sponsors tourist trips to the North Pole, via great ice breaker ships. Hearty souls can take a quickie dip directly over the pole. Long ago we honored the first man to fly over the pole.

In the late 18th century with all the great bodies of water identified, exploration began focusing more carefully on land masses and communities inland. When the English ruled the American Colonies they became interested in the lands beyond the Alleghany Mountains. To establish claim they knew they had to have it surveyed to document any claim. They found a young fellow still in his teen years who was willing to do the work, learn the processes, and risk the dangers. His name: George Washington. Young George provided the first official support for claim of the Ohio territory for the British. Later and before the American Colonial Revolution, Washington as an officer in the British military, was sent to the Ohio territory to fight Indian wars that were supported by the French, who were repeatedly in warfare with the British – at home and abroad. Washington was believed to have both leadership skills and knowledge of the area from his early surveying experience there. The venture, though deeply troublesome, began fame for Washington that ultimately made him first in the hearts of his countrymen.

In 1803 the American President, Thomas Jefferson, commissioned the Lewis and Clark expedition to explore the headwaters of the Missouri River. The underlying reason for the expedition was not only to chart the land for possible agricultural development but also to find a navigable water way to the Pacific Ocean. They did not find the water way, but they charted a route through the Rocky Mountains to the Pacific Ocean. They worked their way through harsh weather and sometimes hostile Indians without losing a man. One died from natural causes, and Sacajawea, the Indian maid, cared for her infant during the journey, but was vital to the project – especially in travelling through Indian territories under Indian control. That control did not include documentary claims. Casualness about land claims proved to be a major mistake for the native people, both in American territory and on other continents. By the time they learned the white man's system it was too late. They had no official survey or court house.

President James K. Polk was known as the Great Expansionist. He is remembered for keeping his campaign promises for national territorial expansion – the western movement. Polk stepped up the momentum, as Lincoln later did with the gift of land to American settlers willing to farm the measured land areas. During Polk's term, surveys and explorations of unknown territories were commissioned for the Great Plains west of the Mississippi River. Railroads to the west were projected and surveyors commissioned to find the best routes. As George Washington became a key surveyor of the Ohio territory and the Ohio River, his tradition was enlarged with surveyors finding the best routes westward. This was vital for future planning and extensive in the settlement of the west. We now know that they found the best routes, and warned about possible routes that might be dangerous because of weather but shorter in distance. Some wagon trains disregarded their warnings, and settlers lost their lives. The most famous of these was the Donner party relying on a vague surveyor's report of a possible pass through the Sierra Nevada Mountains into California. The surveyor was General John Fremont who explored and established the Oregon Trail. His trail route was highly regarded in the move westward. He later ran for nomination of the Republican Party against Abraham Lincoln.

The decades following the Civil War brought with it industrialization and demands for better transportation. Roads, railroads, bridges, even towns and airports needed to be situated in strategic locations. All these objectives required the services of explorers, and colleague surveyors to identify and scale out thousands of sites. Western stories could be told of the frontier professional, who advanced the nation's expansion with a tripod rather than a six gun. Success follows for us when we seek and find order in the context of a search. Surveys brought order to land and society. It contributed to peace and progress. We find some of what we look for and some factors unexpected. We mold them into our experience and sense of meaning in our lives. One of the factors for order in physical exploration is the concept and application of the documented physical survey. One such survey is to chart land surfaces. That information is life changing.

It is likely that most persons have little or no idea of the importance of the survey process in a developed society. One of the disadvantages faced by the American Indians was that they had no surveyors to map out property claimed by owners. They had no measurements or official storage of data about the vast land in which they became Bedouins. The settlement of Oklahoma is a dramatic experience in which the white settlers, the Sooners, moved in according to the survey records of the land charts to individual ownership. Each farm/ranch was specifically assigned. Such a process ended the problems found in the Indian tribes fighting, even among themselves, on land claims. There was no record for them that protected boundaries. With the mapping and measuring of the great American countryside it became the largest single project to be occupied by invading settlers and that done in a short time period.

Today mankind is reaching forward to two ends of the created spectrum; the universe and the atom. The demand for space travel, for citizens who can afford the fare, is just a few years away. Persons are planning to go in to space as though they were traveling in a modern airplane from one city to another. Space Ports are being designed. At the same time atom smashing facilities have been constructed and in use. Both of these need the services of land surveyors to place strategically the physical boundaries for optimum performance and achievement of purpose. Some of the first residents on a planet in the Solar System will have to be surveyors, perhaps with legal authority to determine who owns the areas surveyed. That will likely be the planning even if there is a United Nations claim attributed to all nations. The anticipation of the possibilities returns us to concepts of exploration and a close mapping of other globes and physical masses for meaning and purpose. Americans were the first to the moon. Do Americans own it? The first to survey it, claim it, defend it and occupy it will argue that they own it. At this writing the matter is an open question, but the American Flag was the first evidence for claim. Perhaps it still waves from the sands in which the American astronaut planted it.

Men and women continue to explore. Some work their way through deep caverns beneath the earth's surface, descending mountain ranges at the bottom of the seas, finding lost cities, or ships that have disappeared. At the root of exploration is the requirement to know and understand the art and science of land and water survey. Land surveying, for the dedicated professional in the field holding desire to see what lies beyond, means to find ways for solving the mysteries, and to disprove myths related to persons and their habitat. Exploration and Land Surveying share parallels in their approach, work and attitudes. Both have an almost fearless attitude in approaches to resolving related mysteries and to adapt to the truths found in nature no matter where they may lead. Even space travel depends on faithful mapping of the material world. The ancients used space and the stars before they learned to map the world, and so to understand that world in time, seasons and navigation. They learned to map the land outside the doors of their homes for better life that included relationships in society. Nothing has been the same since the discovery of that order. It contributes significantly to peace, progress and prosperity for mankind. Without the process we could not take responsibility for mankind's world habitat.

This narrative impresses me to make some personal observations. I am proud to be a surveyor. In many ways the gratification can be interpreted as an objective passion belonging to one's calling for his or her life's work. It registers firmly for me when I am enabled to help a family trust to rightly and legally divide their land to heirs, or it may be to hurry to the aide of a widow so to defend her property with evidence against an intimidating, encroaching, insensitive neighbor. It offers satisfaction to serve in protecting rights and contribute to respect for social order. In strong affirmative ways, the field offers opportunity for me and my colleagues to observe magnificent scenery of earth and space, gaining appreciation for the mystery of life and nature. There is born forceful motivation to search for what lies beyond, to solve the mystery ever recurring, and find facts for truth – that may even identify myths, perhaps to dissolve some of them, or give credence to others. There is mystery in it, as there is in all good things.

It is a satisfying and noble profession that may run under the radar of the public watch. The general population has little understanding, even awareness of the meaning and importance of land surveying. When driving down the street, a driver senses no interest in the fact that the street was mapped by a surveyor or it would not be there. Or, in buying a home, he might know the builder, but not the surveyor who had to be there at the beginning to determine the length and breadth of the properties in the community.

Generally, surveyors are not interested in public recognition. A competent surveyor simply wants to get it right. He does not permit margins of error. He wants to serve the public good, with exactness in his contribution, and thereby not only to make a living but also to feel the adventure of it all. Most surveyors find the inner satisfaction of their work is sufficient award.

Any profession is noble that meets the needs of society. However, a person feels a bit extra in telling the story of what he does, and in the telling leaves a narrative of how to give meaning to life by doing the noble thing well as a servant to others. For the surveyor, it has to be exact. In searching history one is impressed by some of the work of those upon whose shoulders the modern person stands. I follow those who have gone before and find creativity in the tradition, the venture, and the service. One learns to follow uncharted lands, uncharted for him, and so to replicate what forerunners have done, a worthy thing to do in each generation. Do what others may have done for their generation, but must be done again in the same creative spirit. Ours is new, proof of what has gone before, and even the land changes becoming new for changing generations. The world is always a 'changin.'

On occasions I am asked what do surveyors do? Do you work for the County? I see surveyors in the middle of the street taking pictures, why do they do that? Where does your work originate? The City? County?

It is common in social settings, if one takes longer than a minute or two to explain something, audience attention strays. Surveying, in its proper context, can't be adequately explained in so limited time span - especially from someone who feels highly engaged with it. I have wrestled with attempting short explanations but failed. Once at a meeting with other business owners where they required each person to stand and give a one minute explanation of their business I gave the following: I am a Land Surveyor and provide such services as Boundary Surveys, Lot Line Adjustments, Parcel Maps, Topographic Mapping, ALTA's, Construction Staking, and Elevation Certificates. To which truncated statement the next business owner stood and said Boy! That was a lot of acronyms! My statement, although correct, did not inform my listeners at the level of their perceptions and interests. Perhaps this writing will accomplish some of the communication for me. At least the story told helps provide closure for my life, fulfilling in person and family, in profession and service, in learning and faith, and in the belief that the telling will help this or that person to believe in the adventure of life that includes the growth principle (improvement) in all that one does in and through a lifetime – if proper attention is given to the venture.

My statement was unsatisfactory in that the laymen had no clear idea of what I did than they did before they heard my gibberish. What was meaningful to me was gibberish to them. That seems to be our common experience in our communication with others about substantive meanings. I realized at that event, the general public has little understanding of surveying. Surveyors, like so many professionals, need to inform the public about what it is that they do. It should be personal and as interesting as a crafted story. It has the virtue of facts to support it. It is a part of our history. The Spanish used it to form a number of small countries in South America. The Portuguese used it to make one – Brazil.

There is an interesting tale to be written about the persons who scribble on little sticks, or taking pictures of property from the middle of a street. This volume was an attempt to tell some of the story from a personal point of view. The adventure really happened to me. It awaits others who love nature, who are committed to making the creation orderly for mankind and our dreams. The profession makes it possible for nations to identify their boundaries, and within those boundaries to serve their people. Native peoples lost their lands for the very reason that they did not have an orderly way to map their boundaries and manage them. They didn't have surveyors or social order to document their needs. Some of these necessary objectives rest with men and women who scribble on little sticks with ribbons on them and pushed them into the ground – as children might do in playing a game. What is momentary for them becomes more than a lifetime for others. These sticks become a critical marker in order to place improvements in the correct and legal location - so that the planned building stays within the property or easement lines; or a wall is placed so that it serves purpose and doesn't hinder access, or the parking lot is installed so that it can drain properly, even to show that it must be ordered so to manage winter snows. Among various concerns, our profession is also critical in health and safety for the placing of septic systems or the installation of handicap ramps; for adjustments to lighting whether natural or humanly generated. We are also peace makers in boundary disputes and are committed to objective ways to maintain harmony among involved parties. What we do is vital to an orderly society, providing a valuable and necessary service to communities and individuals.

Understanding what we do is part of the understanding of the humanization process, and harnessing the earth for the benefit of living things.

Most of the surveyors, including me, did not grow up looking and aspiring to be in the field. The profession found them through various experiences. I was wooed to it because of a love for new experiences, and it seemed to offer mysteries of new adventures. I am awed by the rich history of surveyors, and users of surveys, before me like Presidents Washington, Jefferson, and Lincoln. I was further inspired by history of persons who tried to measure the World - explorers such as Marco Polo, Columbus, Magellan, Washington, Cook, Franklin, Lewis and Clark. I thought: I can do that. And, I did, even if it was a bit less dramatic.

Although my stories are modest, not of the same dimension of adventure and notoriety as those before me, they are stories and poems that reflect the everyday life - uncommon to others - in the fields they love. There is enough of the adventure to create a gratifying life and story in the train of the pioneers, and those who follow in their train. My attempt was to write about work, in the spirit of the artist and adventurer - in a way to better explain what surveyors do. There is also some humor. This business is fun. So that the next time you see a surveyor in the middle of the road taking pictures or you see some sticks with pretty ribbon tied on those sticks you will understand their importance and the stories behind them. Then you may smile and feel: I know why surveyors put big sticks by little sticks, and I join in the meaning - and fun.

There is a postscript to be offered here. Thinking about my work and responding to the myriad questions about it there arose within me the desire to tell the story with enough detail, but not too much, to clarify its meaning and processes. It wasn't long until I realized there was more that needed to be told because my work, my professional life, was born out of what I was learning and was becoming. My heart, even as a lad, was taken by whatever was beyond. Had I lived long ago, I may have joined Columbus, or Lewis and Clark because there was something they were doing that belonged to my spirit and mind. So, if the reader has remained with me, he or she will get the story from the beginning of the factors and influences, physical and spiritual, giving meaning to my life and continuity in my business and family – and onward to others.

The telling gives a sense of pleasure to the point of closure in my life – somewhere in a future decade. For those who have felt life to be full and good, for those who would like to offer some courage to others, for those who have loved what they do, and for those who can fold both pleasantries and disappointments into a fulfilled life, this was just one example – my own.

So from my ruminations, and life experiences, I decided to tell the story through the memoir and biographical pattern. I found my work to be so intertwined with my life that I wanted to tell both my personal and professional story in one narrative. It is a necessity emanating from my spirit so to gratify my searching attitude in life and faith. I wanted my family of the future generations to be able to say of me: Oh, that is what he was and did in his generation.

# 15
# Setting the Last Monument

Monuments this surveyor has set quite a few
Some have marked properties that are new
Others are to indicate corners of old
But none are as important as the cemetery has told

Tablets abound marking the final resting place
Information is supplied by inscribing its face
The dates of life and the importance of a name
Permitting the observer to live a moment of fame

Reflections may make a loved one ponder
Bringing insight into life in all its wonder
Trying to find answers to questions of when
To what was, and what could have been

The passerby is intrigued and guessing
Why the stones are marked with such blessing
We can only fabricate what this life once meant
To the good times and the people spent

## Setting the Last Monument

This expert measurer hoped to make a difference
Marking boundaries where owners gained dependence
The map that is stamped and signed
Telling the story of monuments all aligned

But none is as important as the last one of stone
For the hope would be formed in his place alone
That he made the boundaries to the betterment
As they scribe and place his last monument

While gazing upon the stones of monuments
This surveyor hopes there are documents
That reflect accuracy and precision
Showing he made a good decision

-   For life

*This photo was taken when I was four years old with my brothers. Don (Dean) is to left, Robert (Arnie) is in the middle and I of course am to the right. To the untrained eye it would appear that this is a photo of three young boys growing up as trailer trash. But beneath the surface there are telling signs of what I was to become even though I did not see it at the time. Notice the holster around my waist that seemingly was for a toy pistol but in reality it is a scabbard for a plumb bob, while the undersized hooding is a really a surveyor's vest with the typical pot belly that so often accompanies my profession. The two young boys are my field crew and to the left is our survey 'rig.' The rag in my hand is actually a map I prepared for my client. So to reword Lady Gaga's song "I have the right map Baby, I was born to survey." (Actually her song says "you're on the right path baby, you were born this way.) Ok, I took a little bit of liberty here but you get the point.*

*Plaque describing history of Union Hill Elementary.*

*The Empire State Mine which is now an historic park. As a child growing up, I would often spend much of my time "exploring" the mine shafts and buildings. Looking back it probably wasn't such a good idea and feel very fortunate that nothing happened.*